Catalogue

Matthew Higgs and Mark Barrow

MATTHEW Around the time of your first solo show at White Columns in 2008 you stopped working on conventional supports—e.g. canvas or linen—and started working on fabrics designed and woven by your partner Sarah Parke. Can you say something about this shift, how it initially came about, and how it affected your approach to the work at that time?

MARK At the time, I was making stripe and grid paintings on coarse Belgian linen by tracing each grain with small dabs of paint. Sarah was designing striped and plaid textiles for the apparel industry by plugging in colored pixels to a CAD program. There was a moment where we realized that we were working at separate, concurrent jobs basically doing the same thing. So it was not a big leap to come up with the idea initially. Leading up to that first show at White Columns I began to feel restricted by the linen I was using—I could only find three or four different types. Sarah had an old loom from college and I asked if she could make fabric for me. For her, it was an opportunity to do something more hands-on. For me, it seemed like an obvious solution to the limitations of the material. It was a natural progression that rose out of necessity, but it opened up the work to an array of content and eventually restructured how I conceptualized the work.

MATTHEW Over the past five years Sarah's woven fabrics have become increasingly elaborate, essentially artworks in their own right. The resulting collaborative art works, which ultimately remain paintings by Mark Barrow, have an unusual, hybrid identity. Can you say something about the role of authorship in the work and how you negotiate this in your conversations with Sarah?

MARK The fabrics are indeed artworks in their own right and Sarah has her own practice outside of our collaboration. Sarah, in a sense, gives me an artwork to be turned into another artwork. In the final work there is a layering of each of our labors. But for me the *idea* is most important. Sarah is designing the fabrics to meet a concept I have. Ultimately, I am responsible for the finished object and I have authorship, but she has tremendous creative freedom in her part and her work adds something special to my work. So she is always credited. As we begin new projects, there is a continuous negotiation and there is of course the possibility that our roles will change. Sarah's background is in design and she never had ambitions to pursue a career in the art world. She was thrust into this new context when we first started working together. Our collaboration perhaps points to the dissolution of some boundary between art and design. The difficult part was that there was no clear precedent for what we were doing.

MATTHEW　Sarah's woven fabrics speak to the histories of both labor and craft. They introduce questions of gender into the practice— as weaving has historically been associated with women's work. How do you reconcile these histories that are inherent to both the material and processes at play in the work?

MARK　When Sarah and I first started collaborating, I was interested in conflating the histories of craft and painting. It seemed like a subversive idea and the history of craft offered an alternate but parallel narrative to Modernism. As this has become a more mainstream idea in contemporary art I have shied away from this aspect of the work and have tried to push it in other directions. The whole notion is too steeped in nostalgia now and in a reaffirmation of the 'authentic'. Similarly, weaving's sociohistorical place is not something I deliberately address in the work. It is not what I find compelling about weaving. Weaving is a beautiful, logical system. The way in which it can interact or intersect with other systems is what fascinates me.

MATTHEW　More recently you have started to create computer assisted drawings of the paintings—works that function almost like maps or diagrams of the painting's painted surfaces. The drawings seem to relate visually to the punch cards we associate with both the weaving process and also early computer programming. What is your relationship with technologies—both old and new—and how do they inform the work?

MARK　A consistent theme in my work is trying to figure out how we can know or understand something. A rational approach is to examine the components that make up something. We see this in fields like science and technology all the time. Focusing on the smallest elements of a painting is similar to looking at what molecules or atoms make up a substance. It is also a way to create points of equivalence across various contents. A loom, a computer, and a painting, are all complex systems made of simple, repeated elements. I realized that I could draw relationships across mediums and ideas by paring everything down to their most basic components. The drawings are a sort of map or representation of weaving language, digital language, and the language of my paintings compressed into a single layer. All three of those things are based on a Cartesian system so it makes sense. This idea of breaking things down into their basic elements was also the impetus for the *Redaction* project, a book I am making from appropriated texts and images along with a table to display it.

MATTHEW   How do you think about your work in terms of its historical trajectory? Clearly the paintings aren't ironic. They don't fall into the self-reflexive category of painting-about-painting, yet at the same time they aren't examples of a purely modernist project?

MARK   I think if you don't view Postmodernism as a complete negation of Modernism, but as an extension of it, then there are a lot of possibilities. By reintroducing subject matter and coding everything with meaning Postmodernism created many ways to make something new. In our current hyper-networked culture, where everything is fluid and there are fewer boundaries, there is even more potential for new perspectives. However, an artwork only makes sense in relation to other artworks that exist. So if you look at my paintings you can trace things back to different ideas throughout the history of abstraction, but I am also trying to make something relevant to the culture I live in. I think this is what has lead to my current obsession with pixels—it is almost unilaterally how we absorb images today. There is a page in the *Redaction* book project where I isolate an idea by Merleau-Ponty: the distinction between "the spontaneous organization of the things we perceive and the human organization of ideas and sciences." Where these two things intersect is at the crux of my work. On the one hand I am interested in phenomenology and the experience of being in front of an object. On the other hand I am just as interested in how experience is mediated by human constructs like RGB or CMYK color models.

MATTHEW   Can you say more about the book project you have been working on recently, and how you plan to present it—i.e. within a functional, furniture-like structure of your design.

MARK   The project is a conceptual piece that takes the form of book. It is called *Redaction* because it is a collection of texts and images I appropriated and also because I alter the texts by removing words. The basic conceit of the book comes from the lin   guists, Lakoff and Johnson: we can only understand concepts in terms of other concepts. To facilitate movement between concepts I try to pare the texts and images down to their basic elements—pixels and words. I also wanted to create the environment in which the viewer would interact with the book so I designed a table and stools on which to present it. The dimensions of the furniture are derived from the dimensions of a standard sheet of plywood. And the furniture's design is meant to emphasize the individual plies of the plywood. The furniture is also a way to showcase Sarah's fabric. Each stool is upholstered in fabric she designed based on ideas in the book about digital color space and weaving.

MATTHEW   Is the book project a kind of coda to the painting practice or do you see it as being more explicitly a part of the painting process? I'm curious as to how researching the book project has subsequently impacted upon your current relationship with the paintings?

MARK   I would say its more a 'Da Capo' than a 'Coda' because everything in my practice feeds back into itself. In rethinking that moment years ago where I was painting dots in my studio and Sarah was designing fabric pixel by pixel on a computer, everything was already there. It just took me this long to draw the connections, to ask the right questions. The book represents similar ideas to those behind the paintings, but in a different form. I didn't have to do much research for the book because I was already thinking about most of the texts and images vis-à-vis my paintings. The book seemed like a more direct or transparent medium for delivering the ideas because it did not carry the baggage of being a 'painting'. Its just thoughts bound together. In this sense, making the book has given me clarity of my own thoughts and in how I approach my paintings.

MATTHEW   You've talked about the dialog between a retinal or visceral experience of art and a more rational, even scientific understanding of the nature of objects. Is this tension increasingly the 'subject' of work?

MARK   Yes. In fact, the book touches on this idea in several texts from different points in history as well how it specifically relates to my practice. It is one of the driving forces in everything I do because it is not a simple binary. Sometimes the two contradict each other; sometimes they overlap. It raises so many questions, I am constantly thinking about it.

MATTHEW   Many of the recent developments in the work—e.g. the use of Sarah's textiles, the pairing of paintings with computer-assisted drawings, the book project, and even the shift into developing functional furniture-like objects—suggest an acknowledgement of the limits of painting in-and-of itself? Is this a fair characterization? And if so, where do you envisage that these developments might eventually lead?

MARK   I call many of the things I make 'paintings' because it is the closest approximation to what they are. But it is just that, an approximation. The same could be said about labeling the *Redaction* project a book and table. I have tried to circumvent this problem with the computer-aided drawings by calling them, *Re-productions* (playing on the idea that I am remaking compositions I used for paintings and that they deconstruct the reproduction process). People have a lot of preconceptions about what a 'painting' is, and it is difficult to shift them. Yes, most of the developments in my work are an acknowledgement of that label's limitations. I hope that the *Redaction* project and *Re-productions* will make people reconsider my paintings in a new way. However, those projects are meant to be autonomous works, not an addendum to the paintings. They are different vehicles for delivering similar ideas. If shown with each other or with paintings I hope they illuminate my practice in a deeper way than individually, but they all raise different questions. That is what gets me up in the morning, trying to find a form for the idea. It is the biggest shift in my thinking in the last five years—asking not, what am I going to paint today? But, how am I going to answer the questions? Painting is an engaging, complex system; I can't imagine abandoning it. At the same time, some questions will better be posed or answered in other forms. Exactly what form those ideas take, we will have to wait and see. I have no preconceptions, and it is incredibly liberating.

Zero..., Milan, May 5 – June 23, 2012

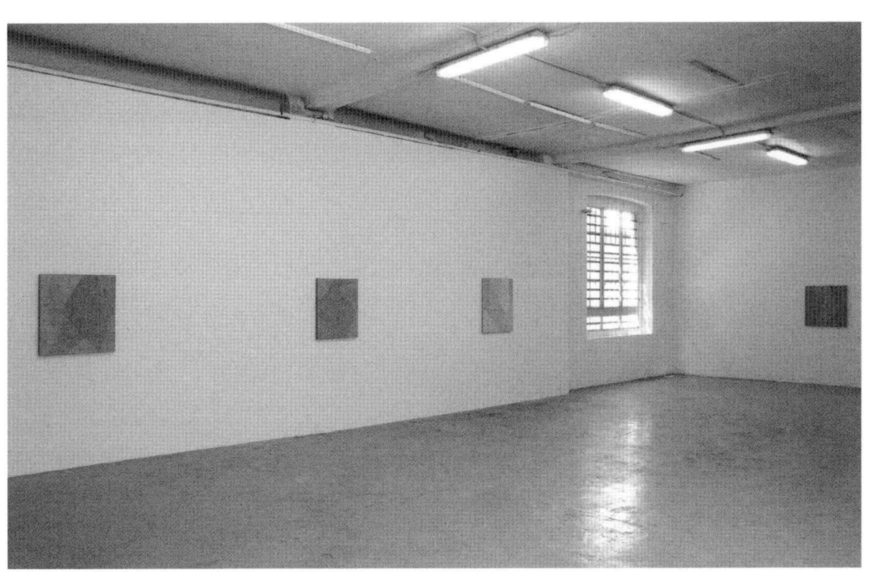

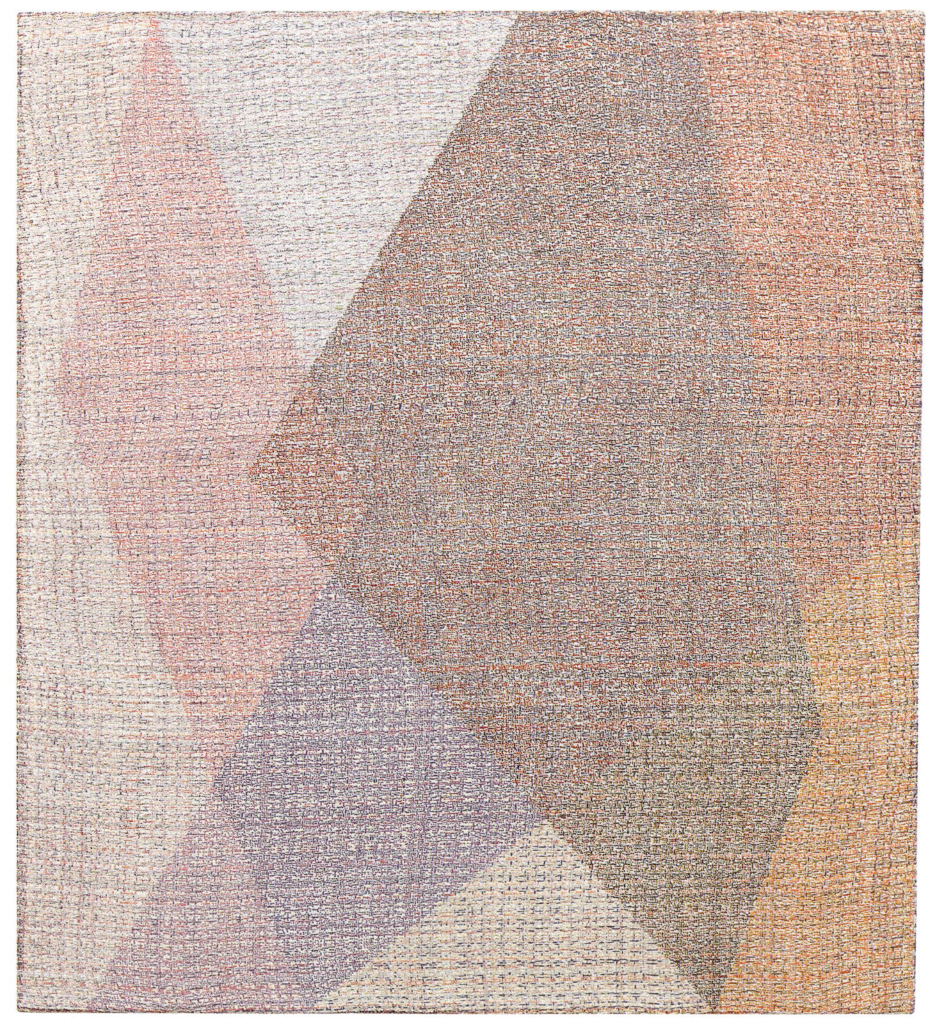

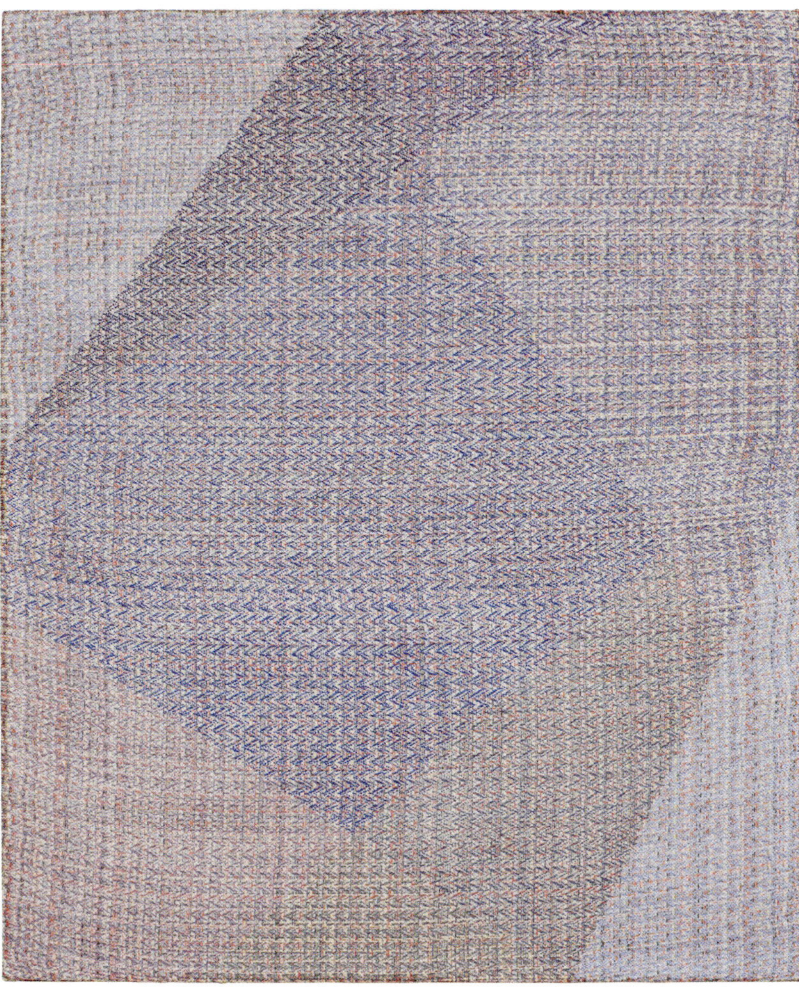

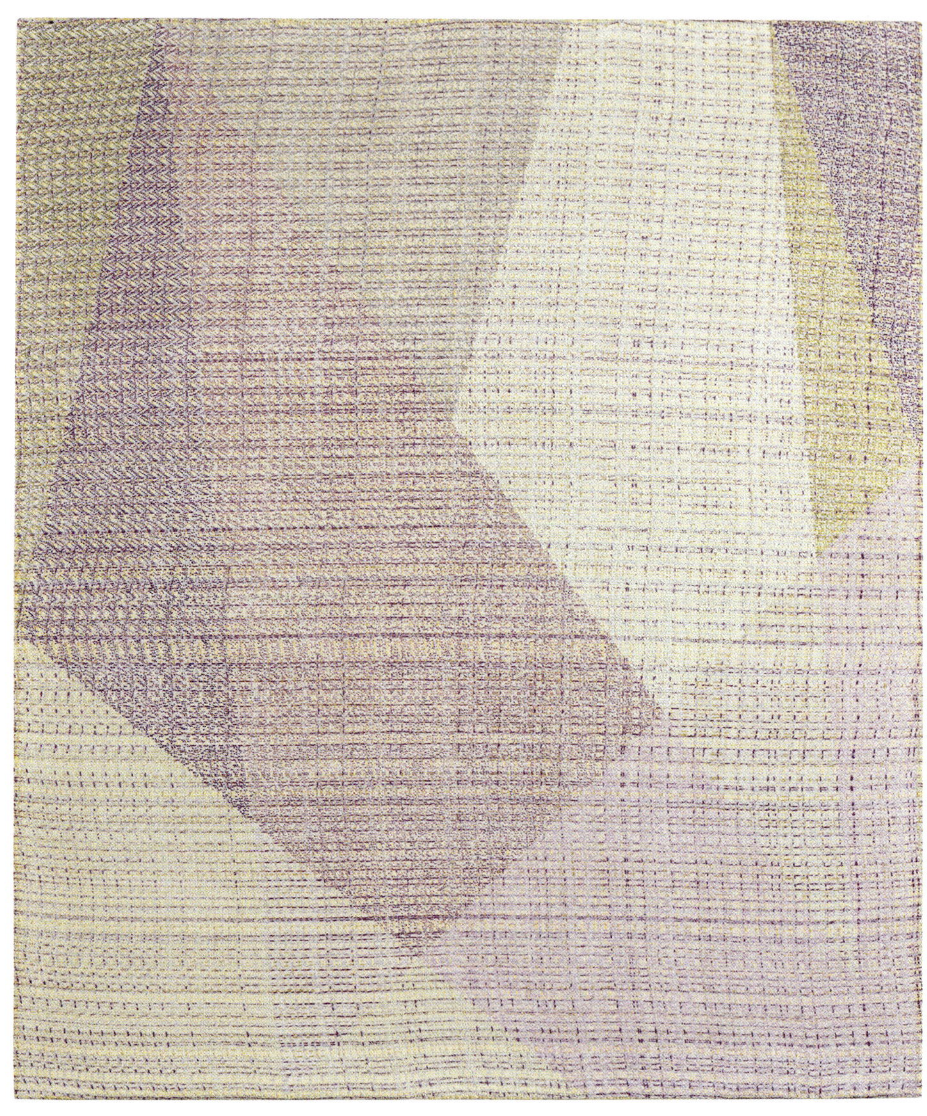

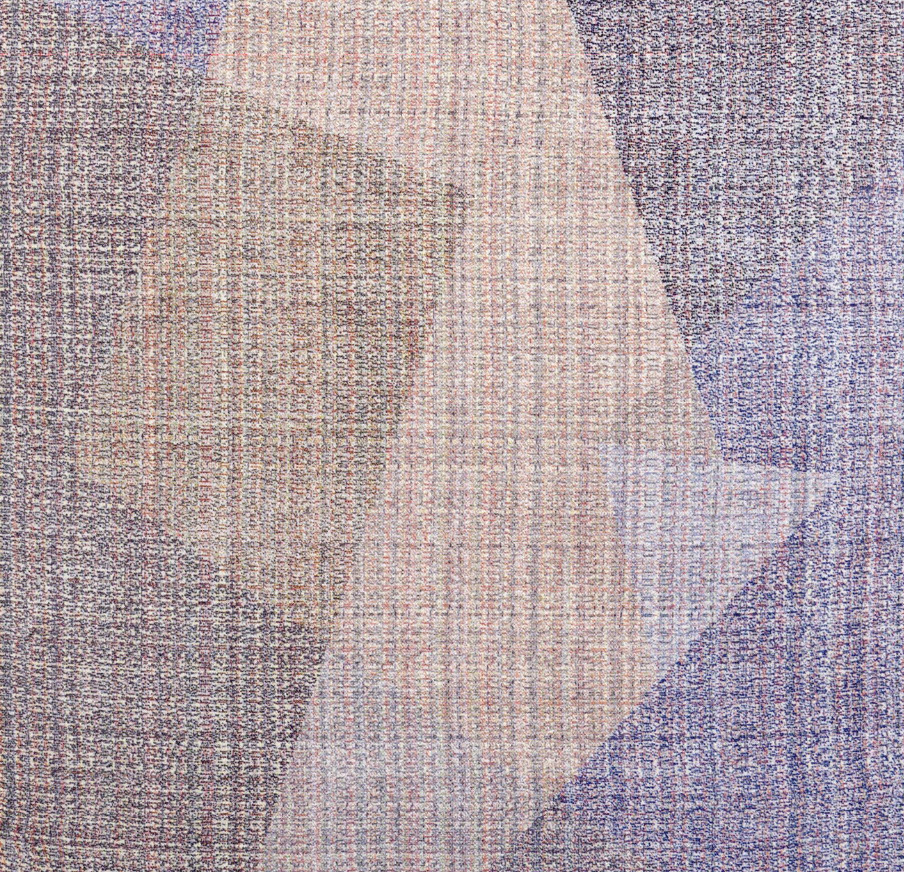

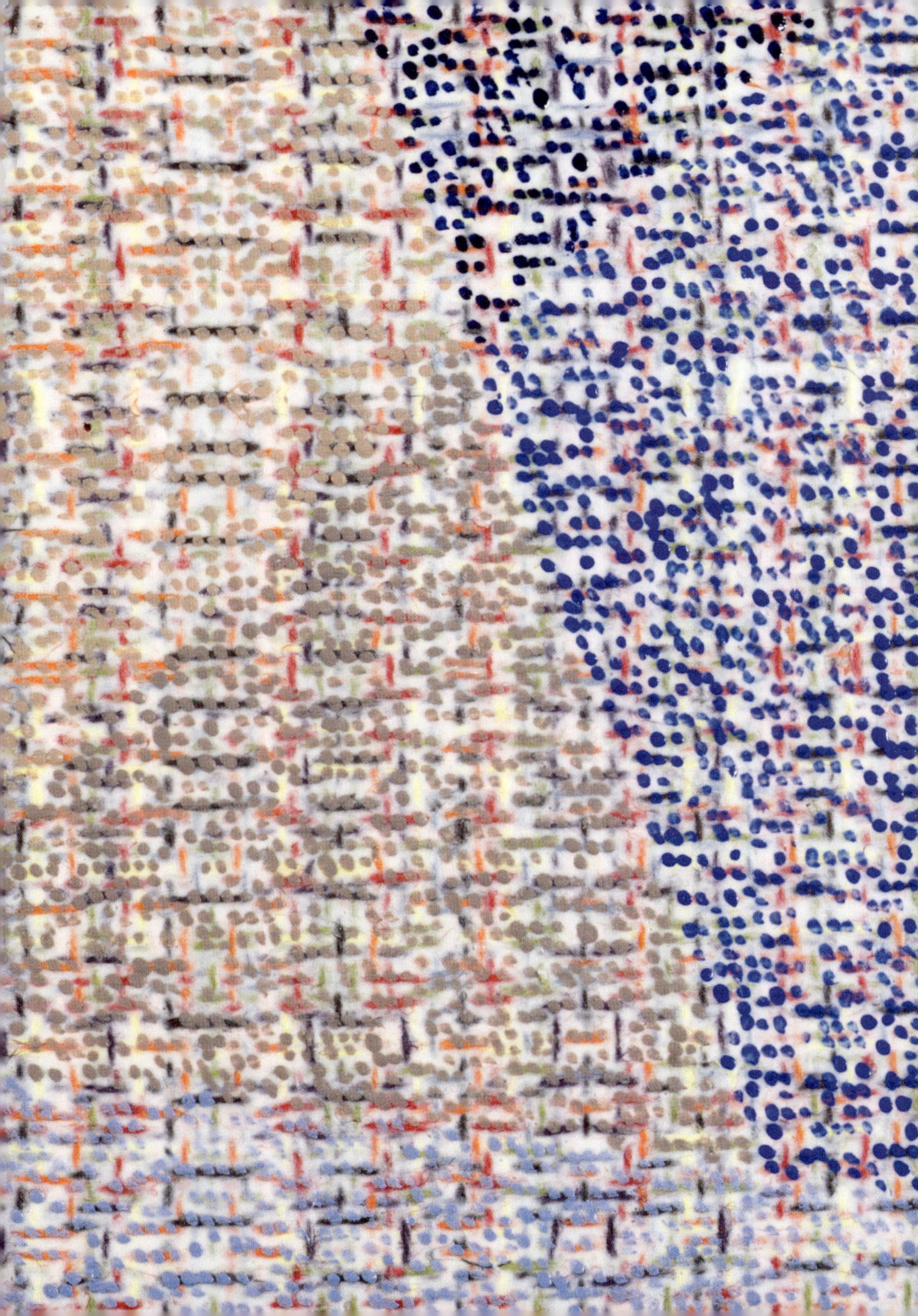

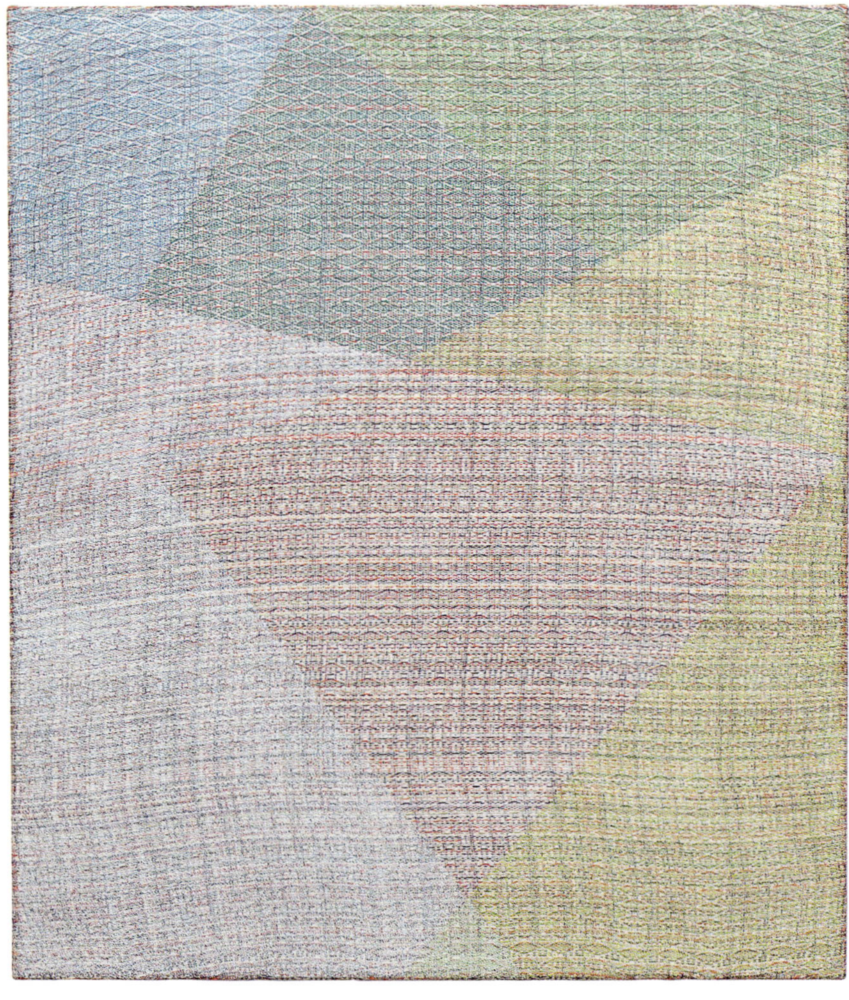

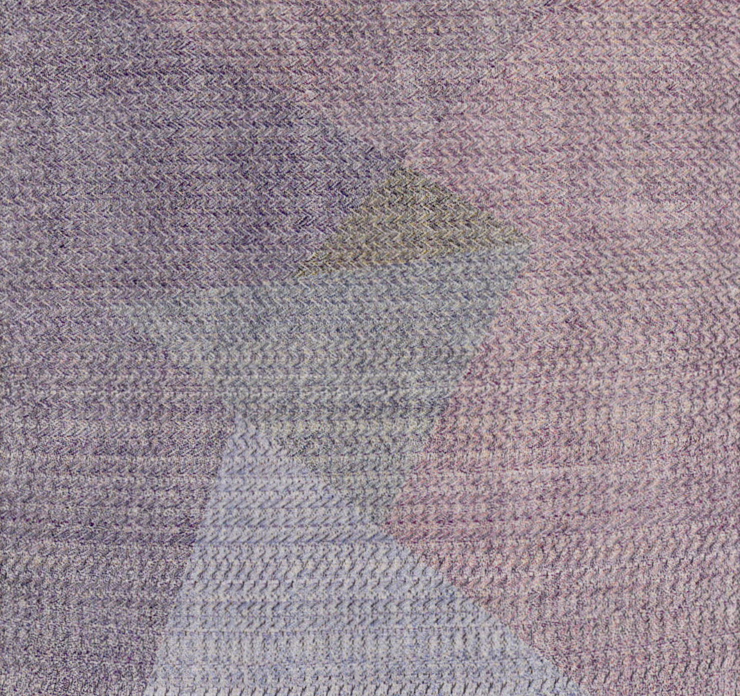

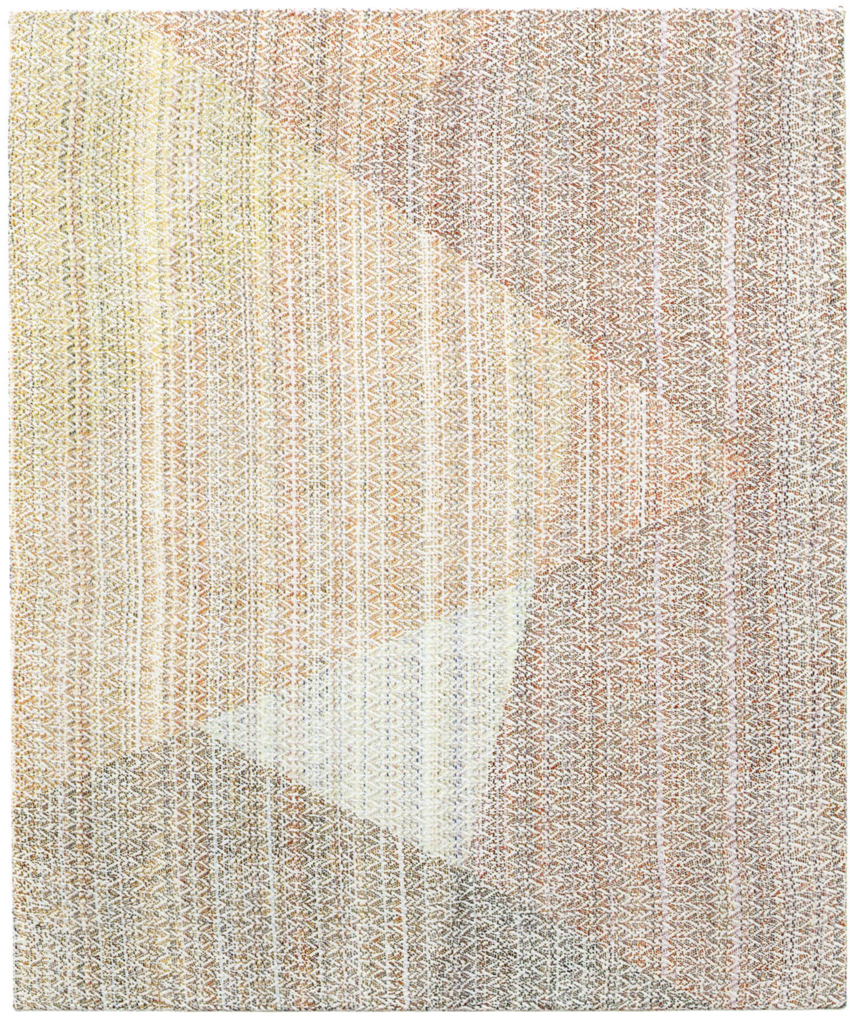

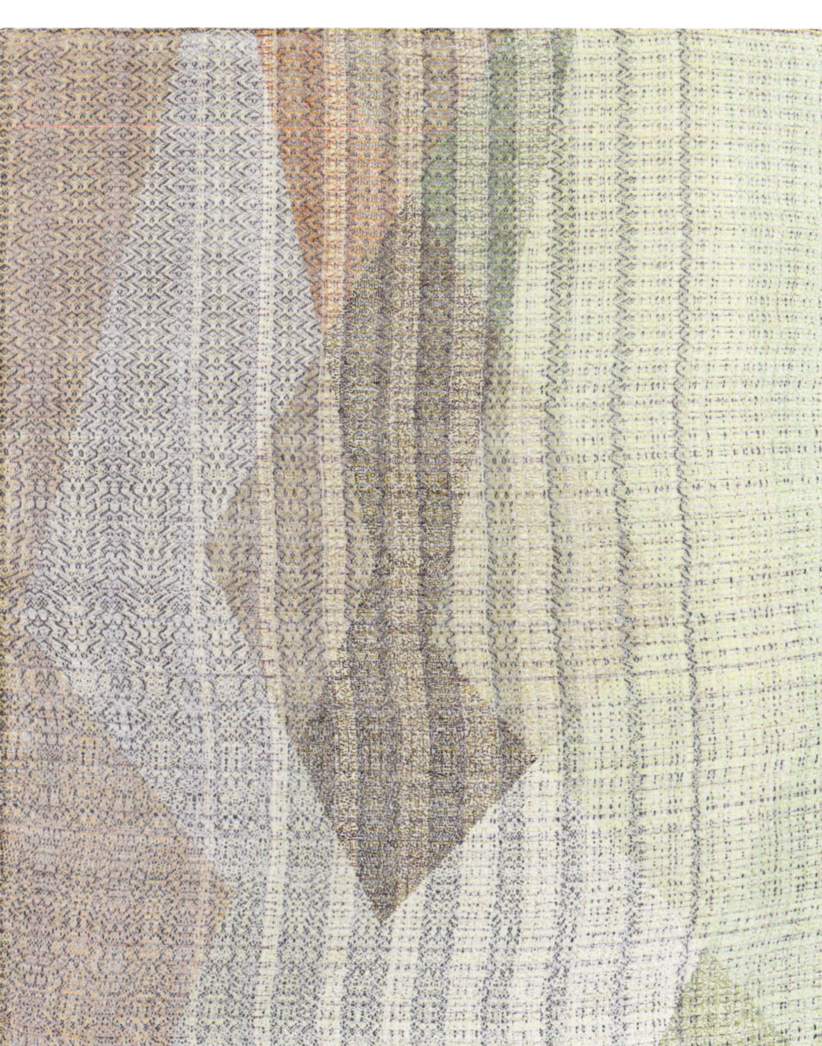

PLATE X

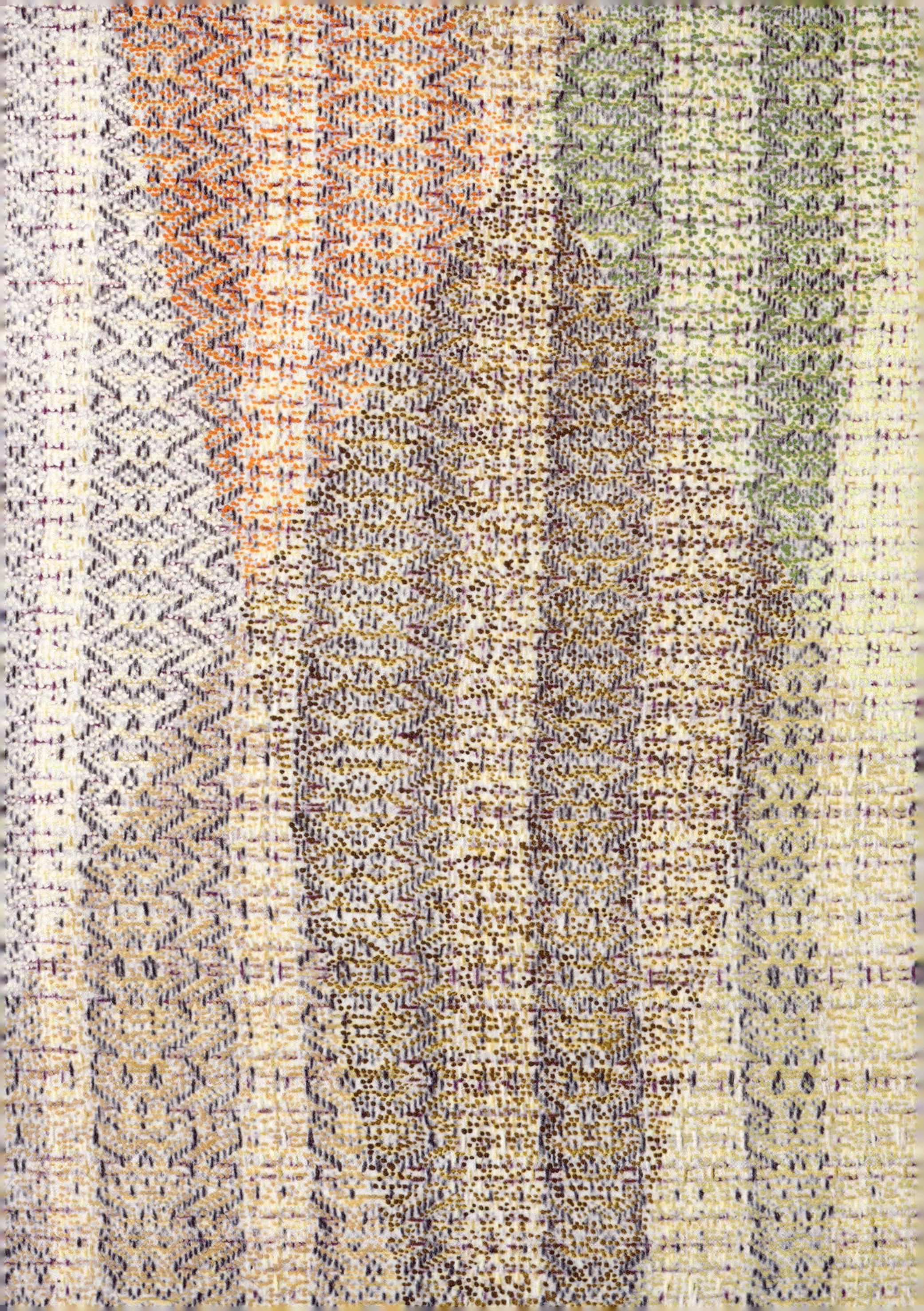

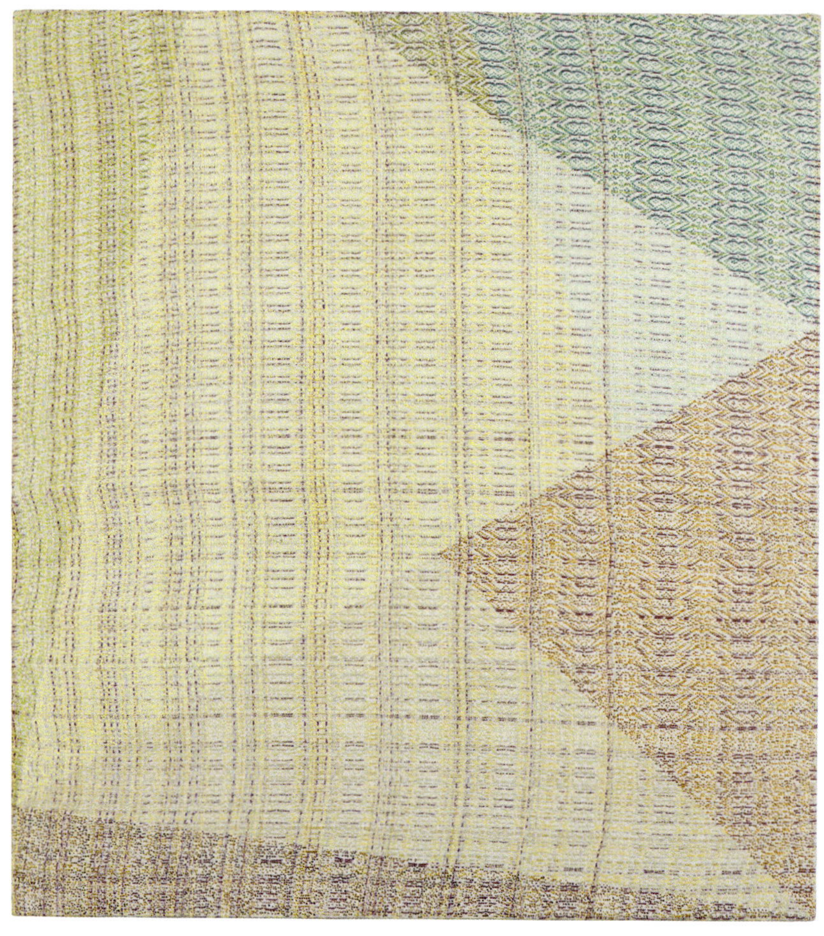

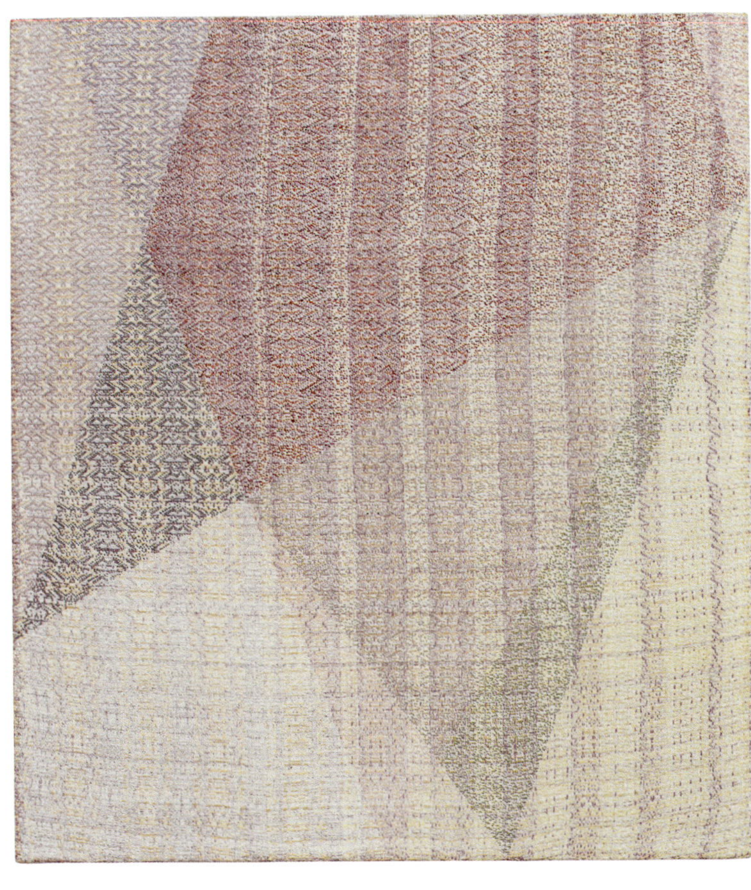

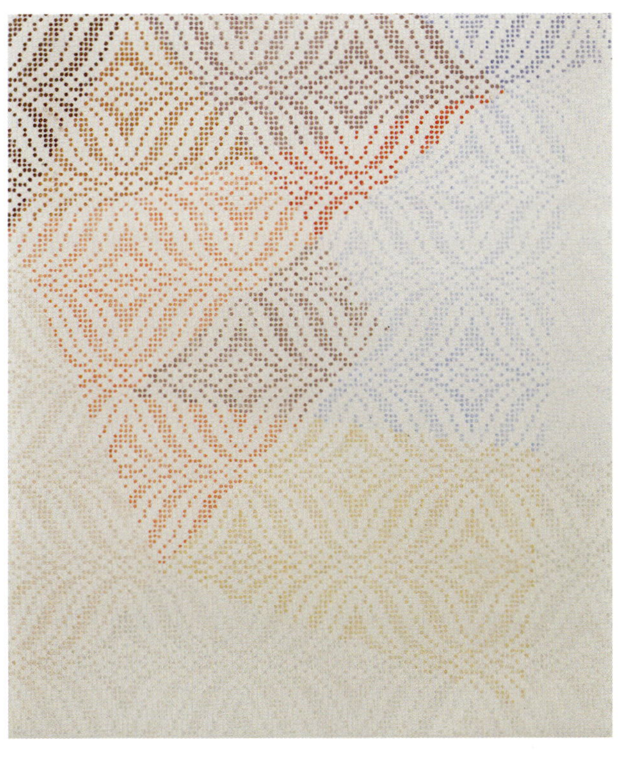

Elizabeth Dee, New York, November 8 – December 15, 2012

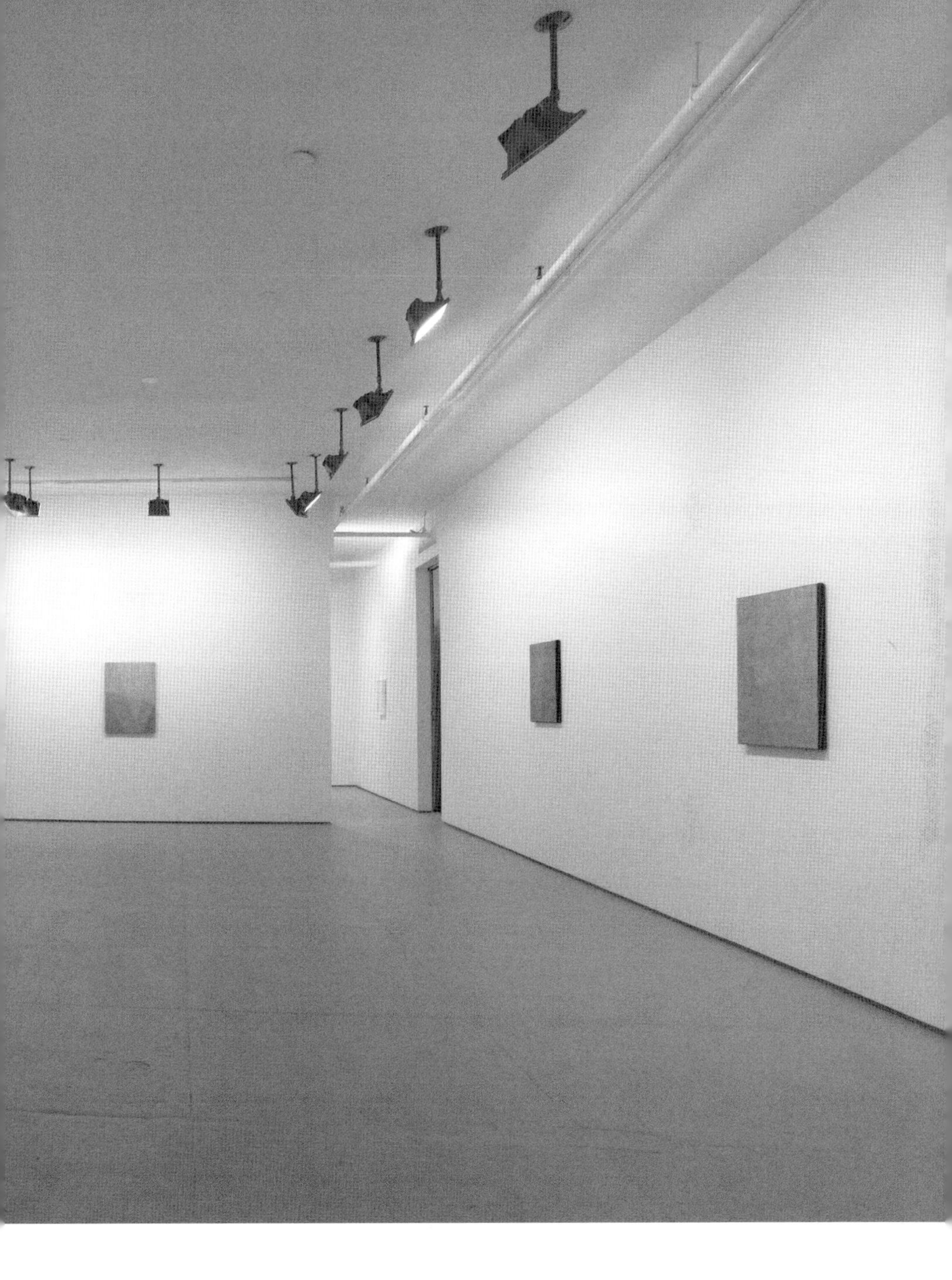

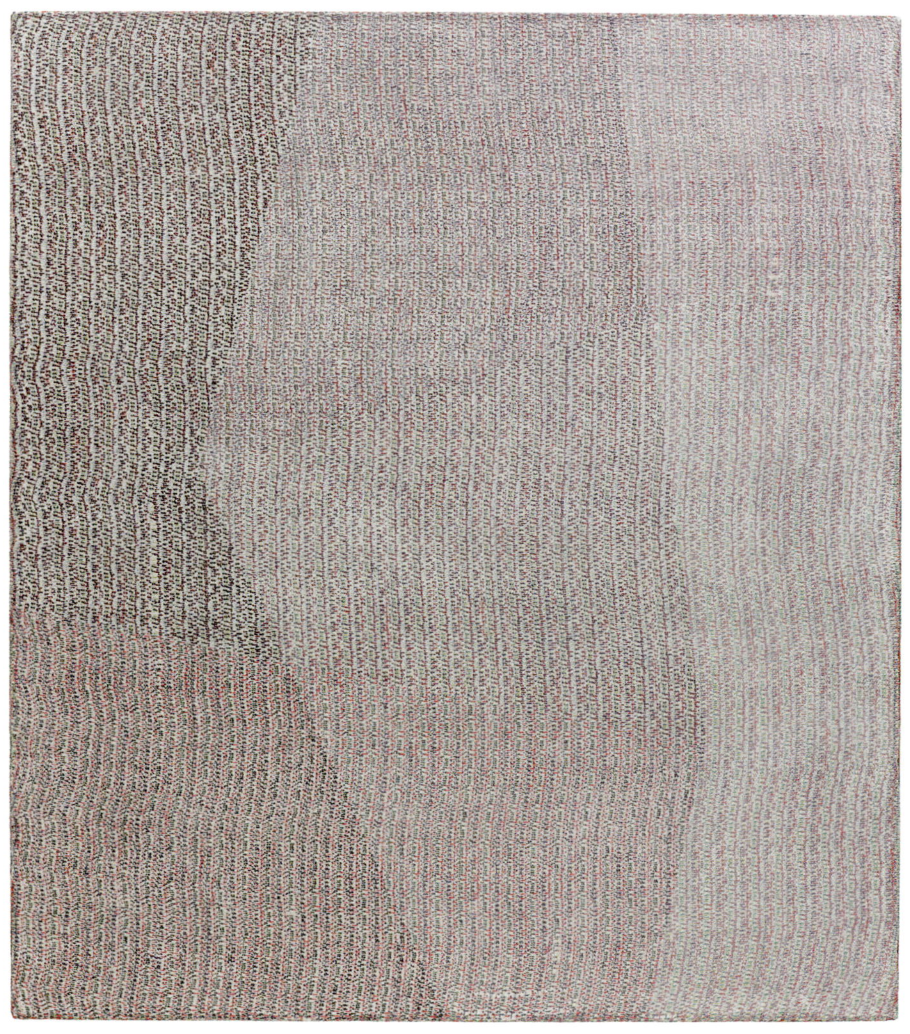

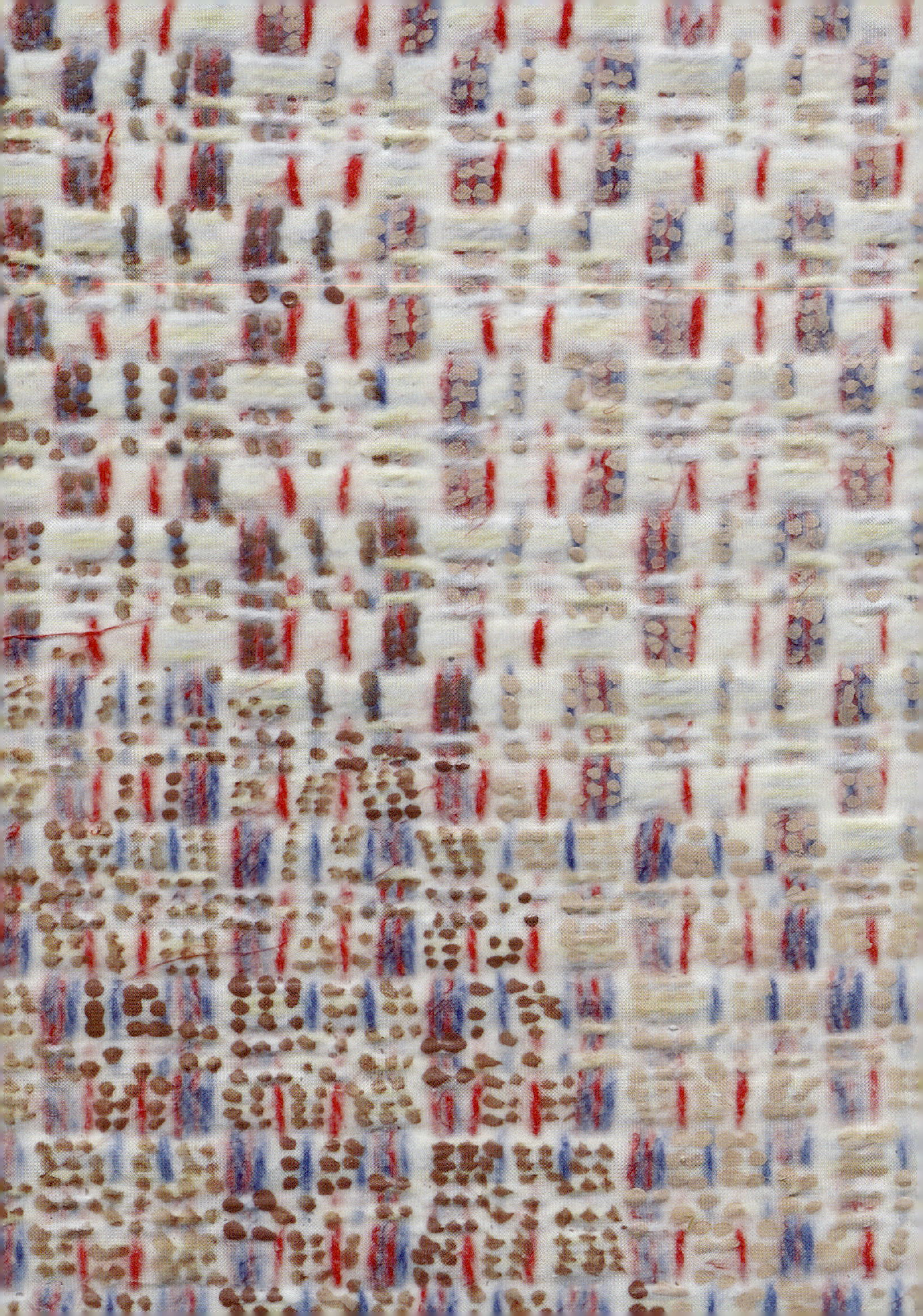

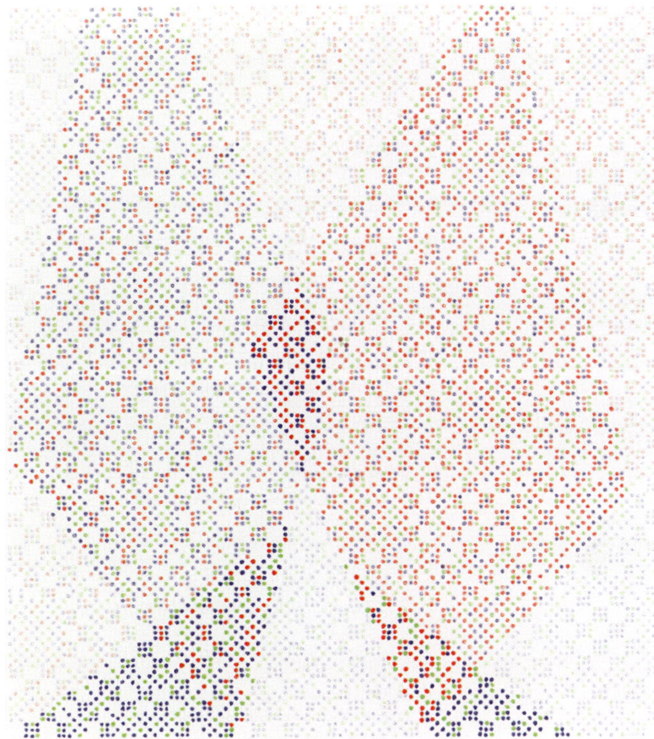

REDACTION

Our conceptual system is metaphorically structured; that is, most concepts are partially understood in terms of other concepts. Metaphors structure not just our language but our thoughts, attitudes, and actions. And are grounded in our experience. Most of our fundamental concepts are organized in terms of one or more spatialization metaphors. Spatialization metaphors are rooted in physical and cultural experience. Our experience with physical objects (especially our own bodies) provide the basis for an extraordinarily wide variety of ontological metaphors, that is, ways of viewing events, activities, emotions, ideas, etc., as entities and substances. All experience is cultural through and through; we experience our world in such a way that our culture is already present in the very experience itself. Metaphors that are outside our conventional conceptual system, metaphors that are imaginative and creative, are capable of giving us new understanding of our experience. If a new metaphor enters the conceptual system on which we base our actions, it will alter that conceptual system and the perceptions and actions to which the system gives rise.

The biggest clue was patterning

it's not just that the individual signs are

being repeated

They were actually putting them in an

order   I
found that those groupings were replicated at different sites

Perhaps this is due to cultural transmission

Or
migration of the same people. Regardless, it's   interesting to see how they
used the art in a   systematic way.

When I talk about   graphic communication, I am using it in the broader
sense.   the symbols appear to be meaningful to
people who were creating them: they were making them on purpose, making
choices.   if they were doing this — whether it's   representing an idea, a
thought, a concept — it doesn't really matter what it actually means, and honestly
we have no clue.   it does suggest   that somebody   could come
along and   understand it.

When it comes to these symbols   They were making
choices about what to put and what to omit.

all of it is geometric.
    which actually makes sense to me.

abstract markings were the first type of expression.

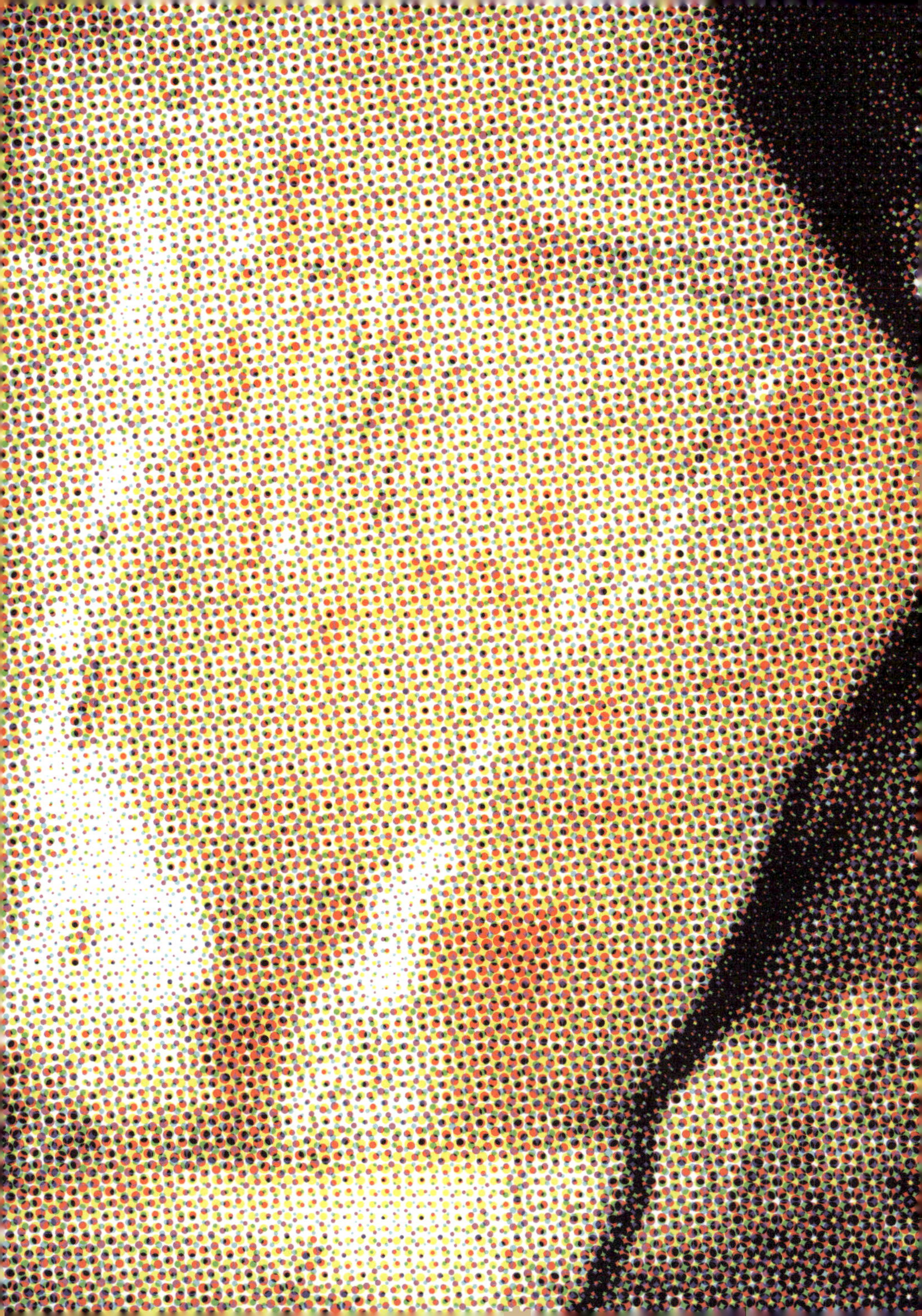

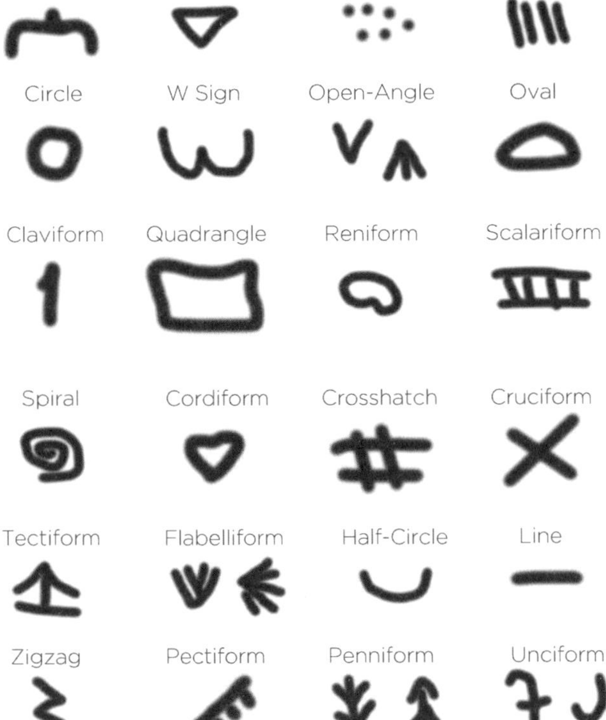

Aviform
Triangle
Dot
Finger Fluting
Circle
W Sign
Open-Angle
Oval
Claviform
Quadrangle
Reniform
Scalariform
Spiral
Cordiform
Crosshatch
Cruciform
Tectiform
Flabelliform
Half-Circle
Line
Zigzag
Pectiform
Penniform
Unciform

We   speak   in   linear   order

      say

            some words earlier
                        and others   later.
                                                            Since speaking is   correlated

                                                                        with   time
                                                                              and
                                                                        time
                                                                          is
                                                            metaphorically conceptualized
                                                                        in
                                                            terms
                                          of
                              space

                  of

                  terms

      it is natural for us   in
      to conceptualize language
                        metaphorically

      Because we conceptualize linguistic form in spatial terms,
            it is possible for certain spatial metaphors to apply
                        directly
                        to
                  the *form* of a sentence.
                                          This can provide automatic

                                                            direct
                              FORM   links
Such links make the relationship   between
                              CONTENT
                                    anything
                                          but
                                                arbitrary.
      The meaning of a sentence

                  can be due to the precise

                  form the sentence takes.

Synesthesia is a hereditary condition in which a triggering stimulus evokes the automatic, involuntary, affect-laden and conscious perception of a physical or conceptual property that differs from that of the trigger.

Orderly relationships among the senses imply a cognitive continuum in which perceptual similarities give way to synesthetic equivalences, which in turn become metaphoric identities, which then merge into the abstractions of language.

perception ⇒ synesthesia ⇒ metaphor ⇒ language

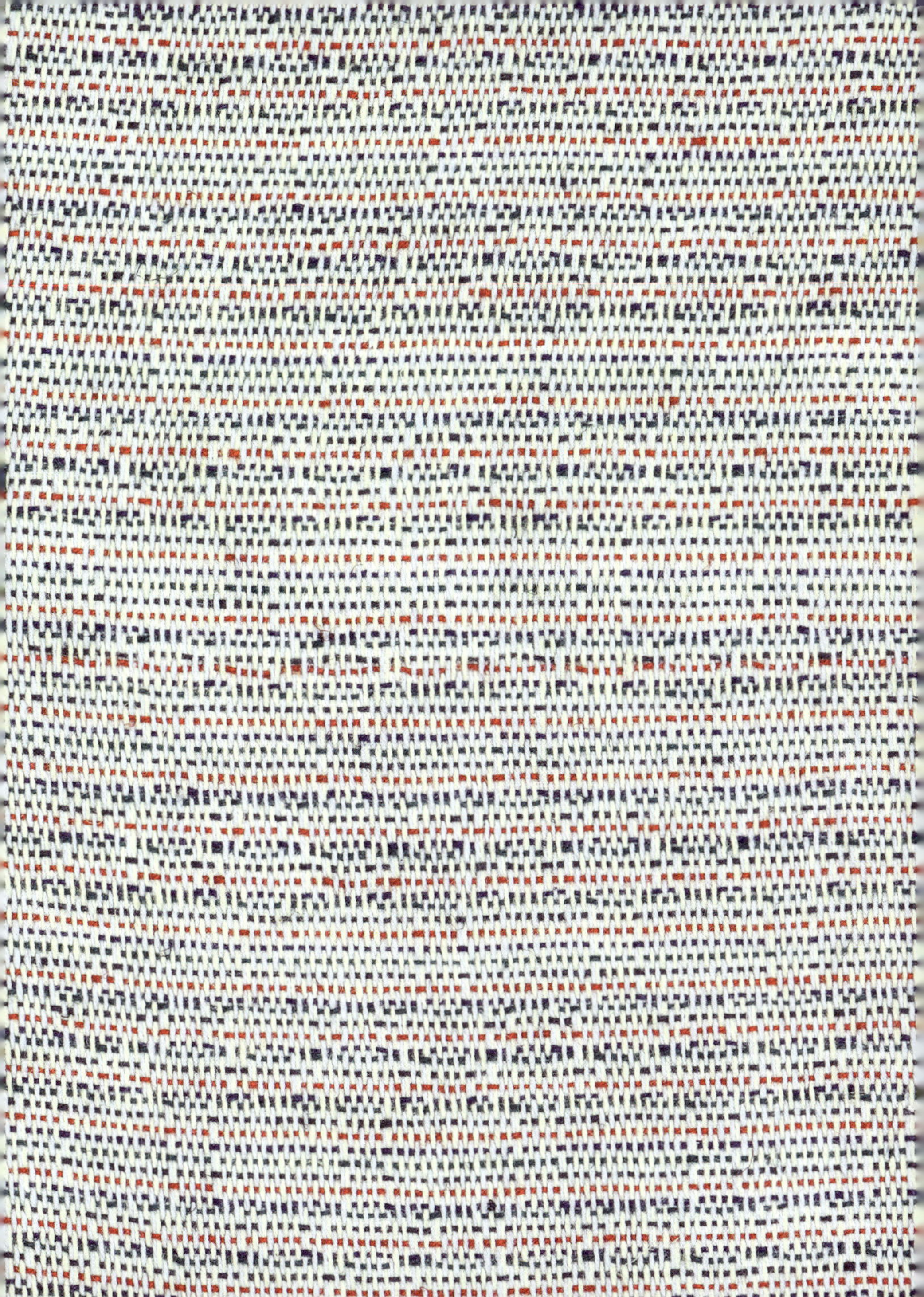

The tapestries   changed shape as they were lying on the floor being photographed. They had been hanging vertically for centuries; when they were placed on the floor, the warp threads relaxed.   The tapestries began to breathe.

It was   expanding

as   contracting

if   shifting

they had woken up.   The threads

twisted

and

rotated

restlessly.

Tiny changes in temperature and humidity   caused the tapestries to shrink or expand

from   from

hour   minute

to   to

hour   minute

A tapestry is a three-dimensional structure.

The tapestry is like water.   It has no permanent shape.

A color digital photograph is composed of pixels. A pixel is the smallest picture element that contains color. The   tapestries are themselves made up of the medieval equivalent of pixels—a single crossing of warp and weft is the smallest unit of color in the image. The woven pixels were maddening because they moved constantly.
it would be necessary to perform vast seas of calculations upon each individual pixel in order to make a complete image of a tapestry. Each pixel had to be calculated in its relationship to every other nearby pixel, a mathematical problem known as an N-problem

This was a math problem similar to the analysis of DNA or speech recognition.

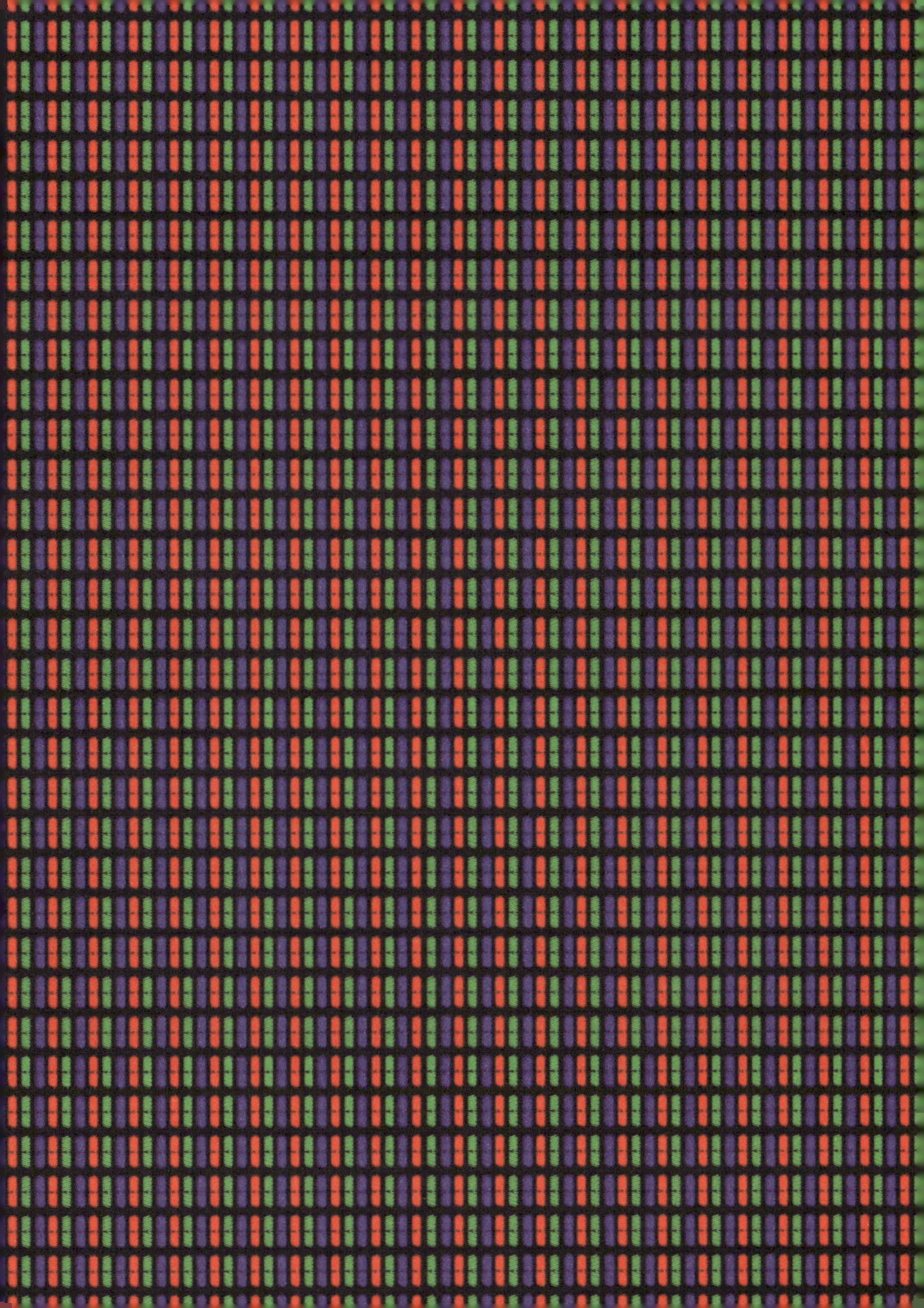

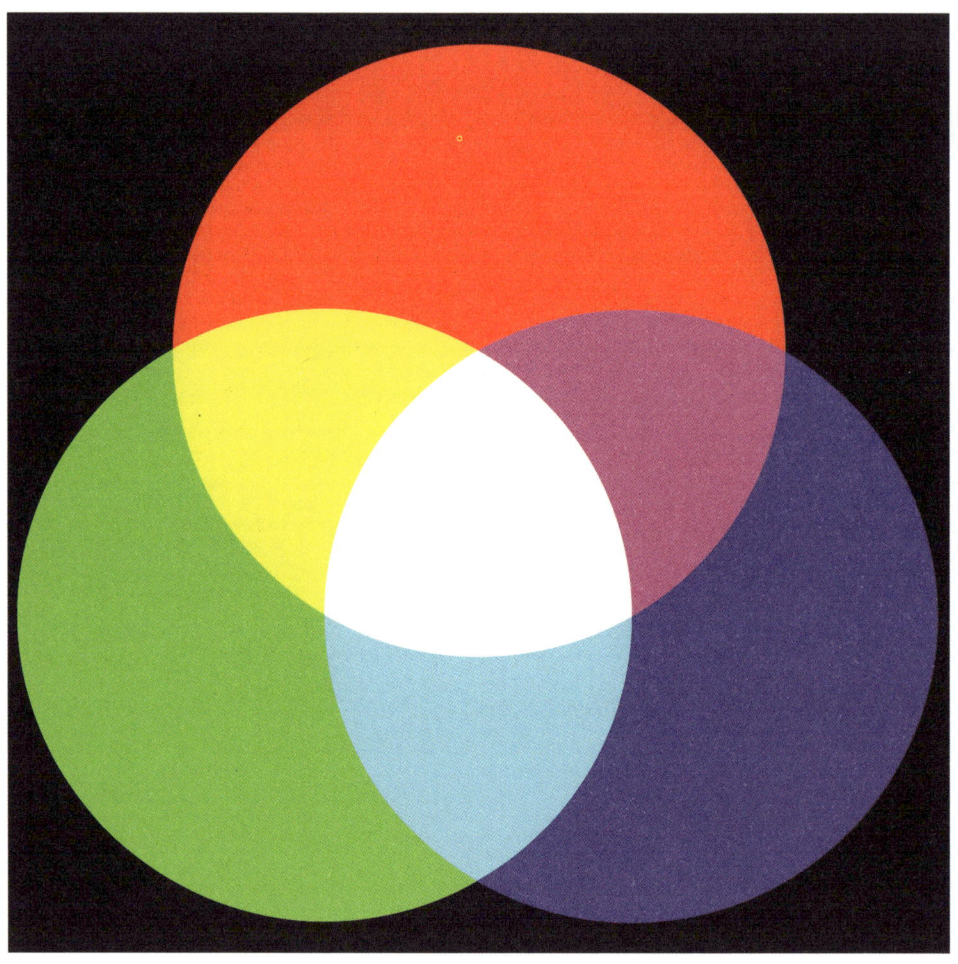

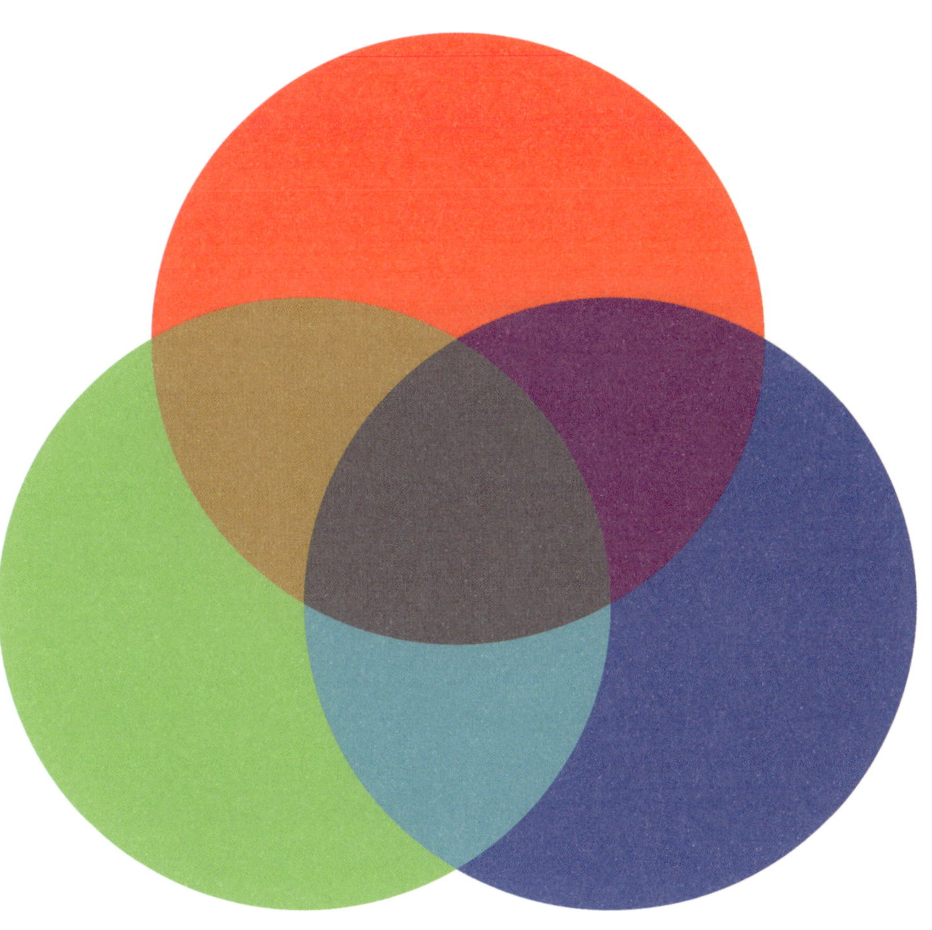

WHITE

Direct Mixture

Projected Light

Optical Mixture

Projected Light

Optical Mixture

Reflected Light

Indirect Mixture

Reflected Light

GREY

He quickly parted ways with the impressionists
Impressionism was trying to capture   the very way in
which objects   attack our senses. Objects were
depicted as they appear to instantaneous perception, without fixed
contours, bound together by light and air. To capture this envelope
of light, one had   only
the seven colors of the spectrum.

impressionists break down the local tone itself

                                                             But at
the same time, depicting the atmosphere and breaking up the tones
submerged the object and caused it to lose its proper weight. The
composition of Cézanne's palette leads one to suppose that he had
another aim.

One must therefore say that Cézanne wished to return to the object

He did not want to separate the stable things which we see and the shifting way in which they appear. He wanted to depict matter as it takes on form, the birth of order through spontaneous organization. He makes a basic distinction not between "the senses" and "the understanding" but rather between

His painting was paradoxical: he was pursuing reality without giving up the sensuous surface, with no other guide than the immediate impression of nature, without following the contours, with no outline to enclose the color, with no perspectival or pictorial arrangement.

He did not want to separate the stable things which we see and the shifting way in which they appear. He wanted to depict matter as it takes on form, the birth of order through spontaneous organization. He makes a basic distinction not between "the senses" and "the understanding" but rather between

the spontaneous organization of the things we perceive	and	the human organization of ideas and sciences

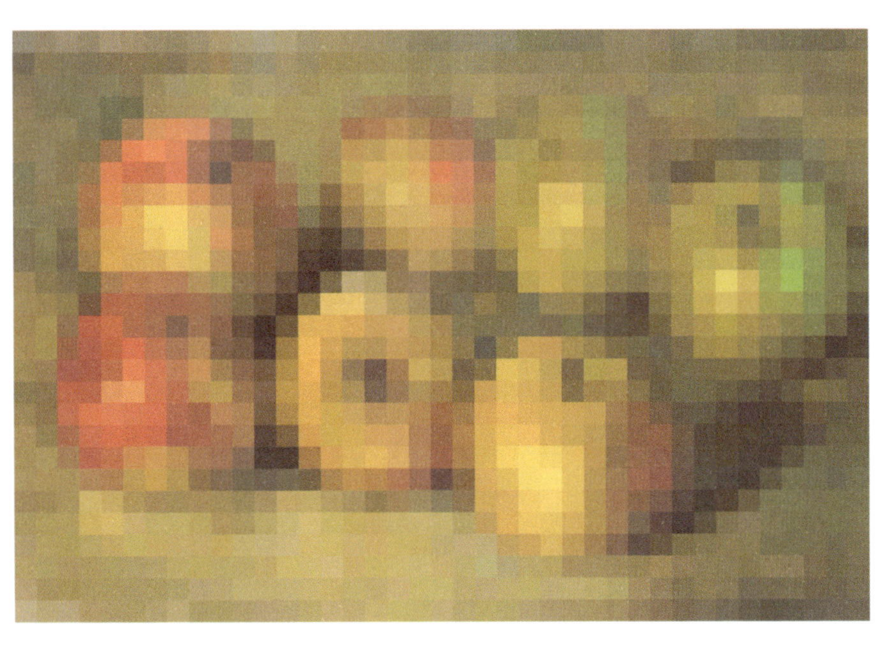

in his painting, consciousness is not torn away from experience.

as if he were the first painter

                                                              But his very desire for the fusion of thought and thinking led him to an insoluble contradiction.   the homogeneity of experience is incompatible with analytical thought.

His obsession with boundaries is not surprising. Boundary is an essential hypothesis of sight. However, when attention is focused upon it, the conceptual assumptions of perception disintegrate   In Cézanne's
        painting process contour becomes the limit *toward* which an object expands. This reverses the given or "natural" relationship of inside to outside, the presupposition of fixed boundaries.

                              This has often been described as ambiguity or doubt, but doubt presupposes the existence of certainty. Cézanne does not. He exposes the dizziness at the very center of decision making. His procedure reveals the vicious circle.

Cézanne's radical legacy   is this question ... How can we ever know what we don't know?

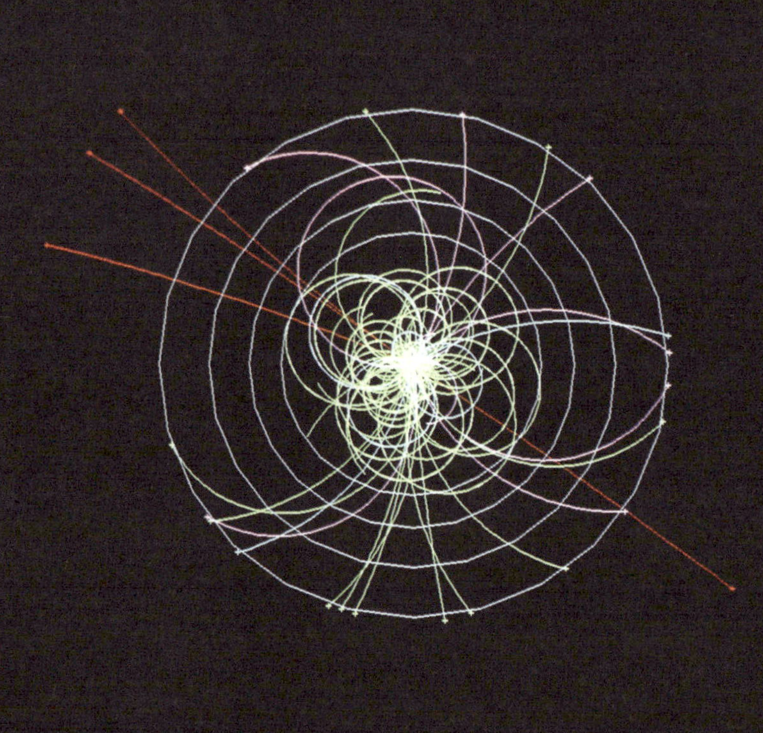

Empirical

spiritual

Stripped of conceptual associations, habits, and references to previous experience, perceptual responses would appear to follow innate laws
The eye responds most directly when nonessentials
are absent.
These means muffle and distort the purely perceptual effect of lines, areas, and colors.

Perceptual abstraction

exists primarily for its impact on perception rather than for conceptual examination.

In "op," the majority of the devices stem more or less remotely from the sort of "trick" designs we have been familiar with from childhood,

Thus the aim of the showing and of the works included is not to evoke a clear direct response from the eye but, rather, to confound and misdirect it,

to confuse the poor, trusting eye and make it see what it thinks it sees but what in fact it doesn't see.

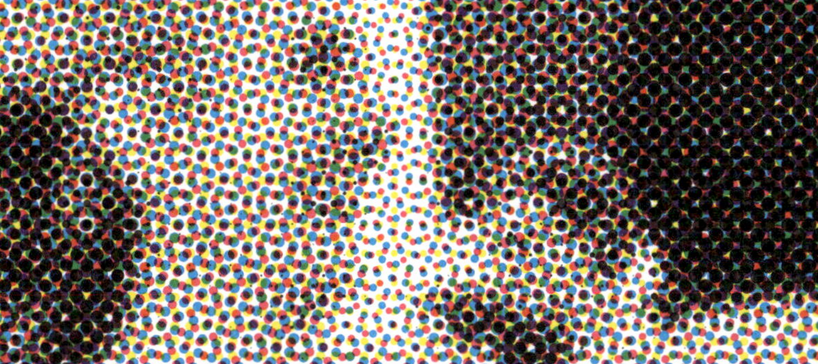

Wassily Kandinsky left behind sufficient writings to indicate he was synesthetic.

He combined four senses synesthetically: color, hearing, touch, and smell.

In the BBC documentary "Orange Sherbet Kisses," Carol Steen and Bill Zimmer are shown viewing Kandinsky paintings.

In the film Bill Zimmer not only points out form-constant shapes in Kandinsky's canvasses but also ones he experiences himself in response to sound.

For some synesthetes, colors induce sound just as sound induces color. Wassily Kandinsky claimed that each color had an intrinsic sound, a relationship he elaborated in his 1912 book, *On the Spiritual in Art.* He later attempted to equate color with Schoenberg's twelve-tone music.

He sought a universal translation among the senses

In 1926, Heinrich Klüver systematically studied the effects of mescaline on the subjective experiences of its users.

He noticed that mescaline produced recurring geometric patterns in different users. He called these patterns 'form constants' and categorized four types: tunnels and cones, central radiations, gratings and honeycombs, and spirals.

Klüver's form constants also appear in near-death experiences and sensory experiences of those with synesthesia.

These elementary patterns of spatial configuration were

induced with mescaline to better understand the subjective experience However, he quickly discovered that subjects were easily overcome by awe and the "indescribableness" of what they saw. The novelty of visions and their vivid coloration captured subject's attention causing them to give way to

cosmic *interpretations* rather than factual descriptions.

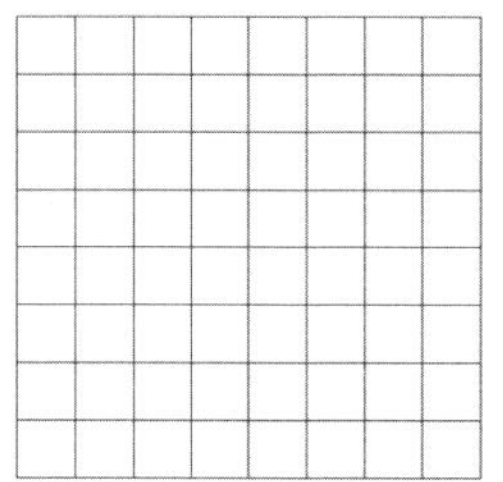 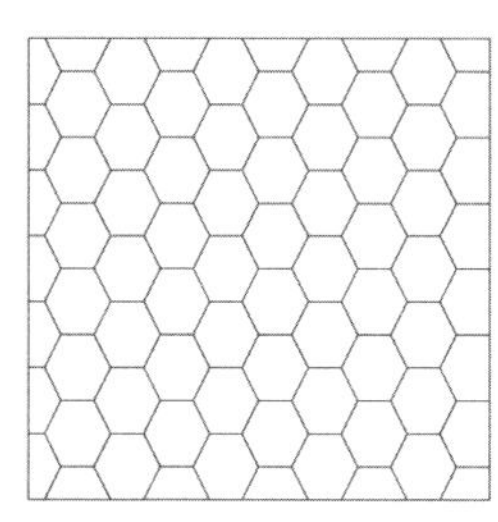 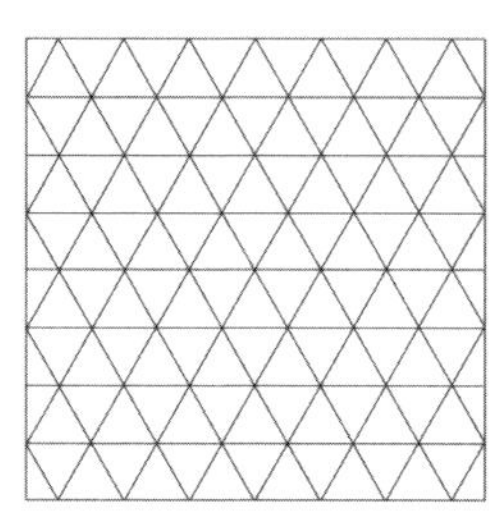

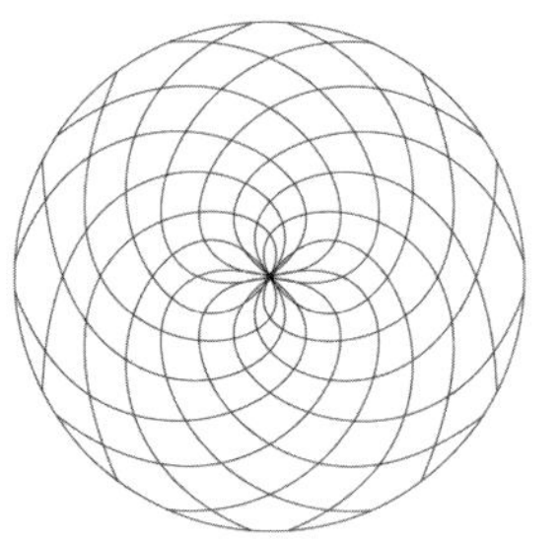 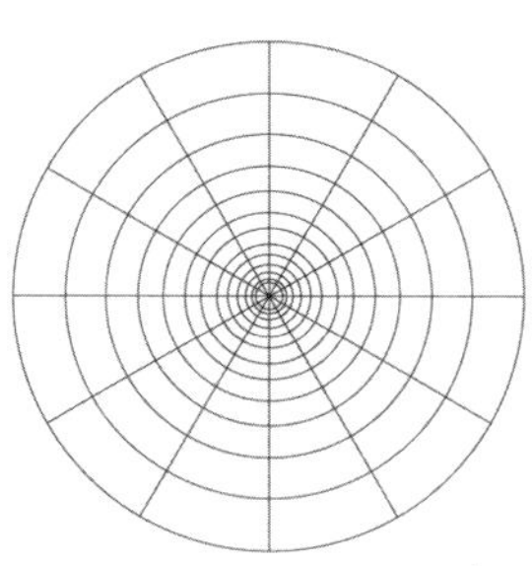

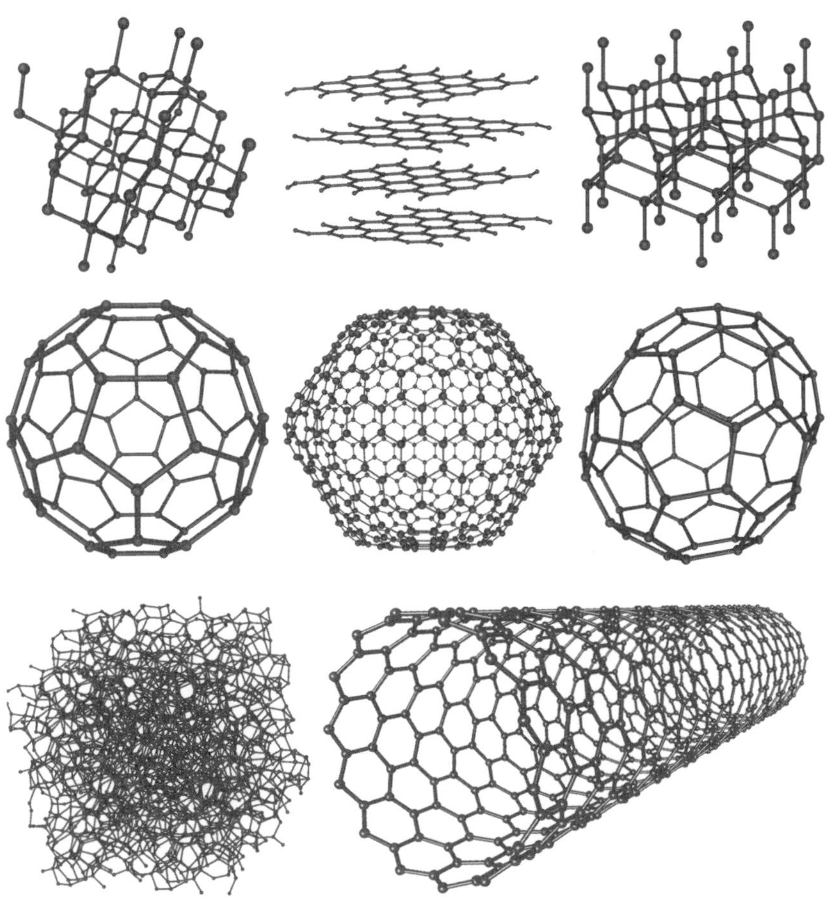

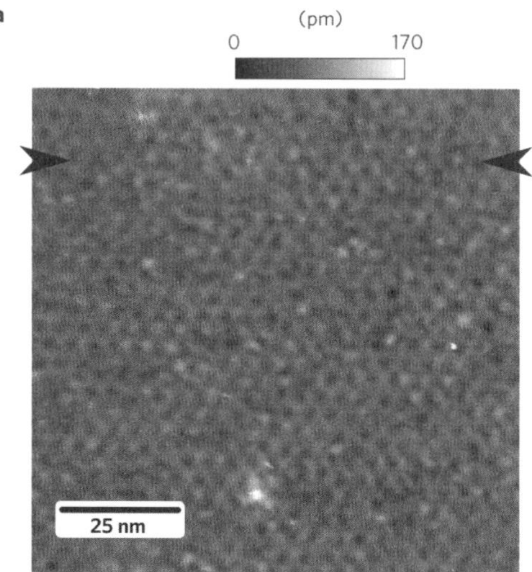

a
(pm)
0
170
25 nm

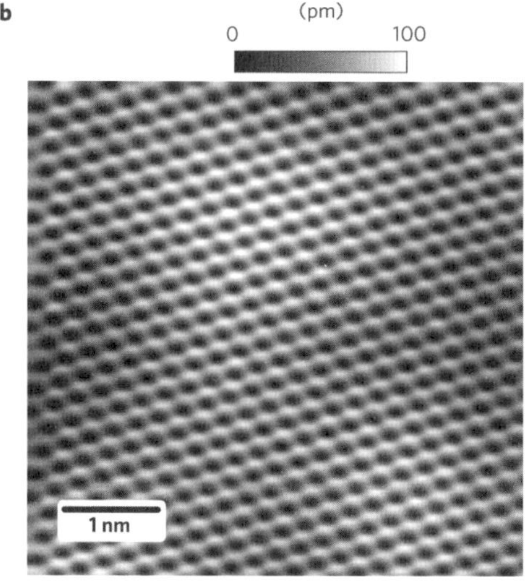

b
(pm)
0
100
1 nm

A formula in mathematics occurred to be the most definite basis from which to work. Taking the cube of a binomial, I approached it in the way applied algebraic problems are approached – by letting x equal one unknown and y equal the other unknown.

In this case, x equaled the first and second harnesses, and y equaled the third and fourth harnesses. Then it was simply a matter of expanding the cube of the binomial and substituting the values of x and y to write the threading draft.

$$(x+y)^2 = x^2 + 2xy + y^2$$

$x^2=$

2 2

1 1

$2xy=$

4 4

3 3

2 2

1 1

$y^2=$

4 4

3 3

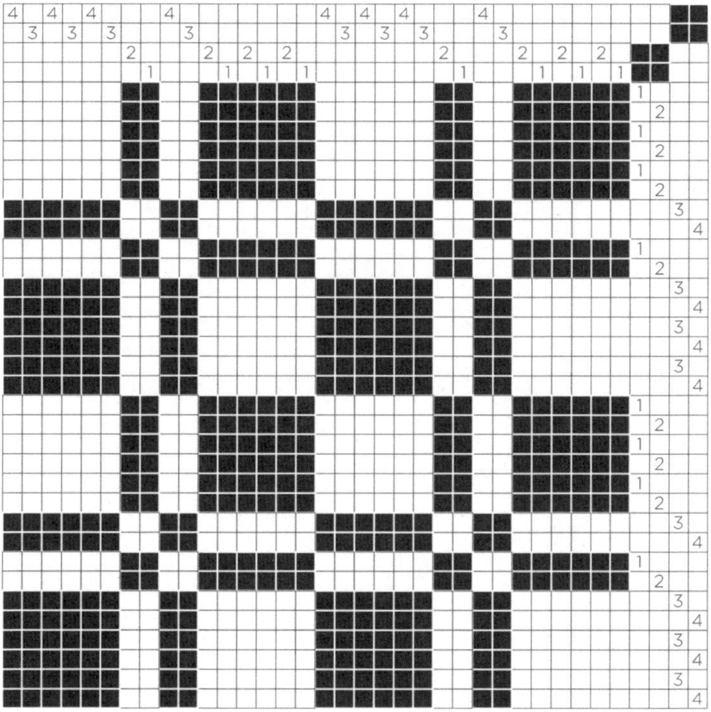

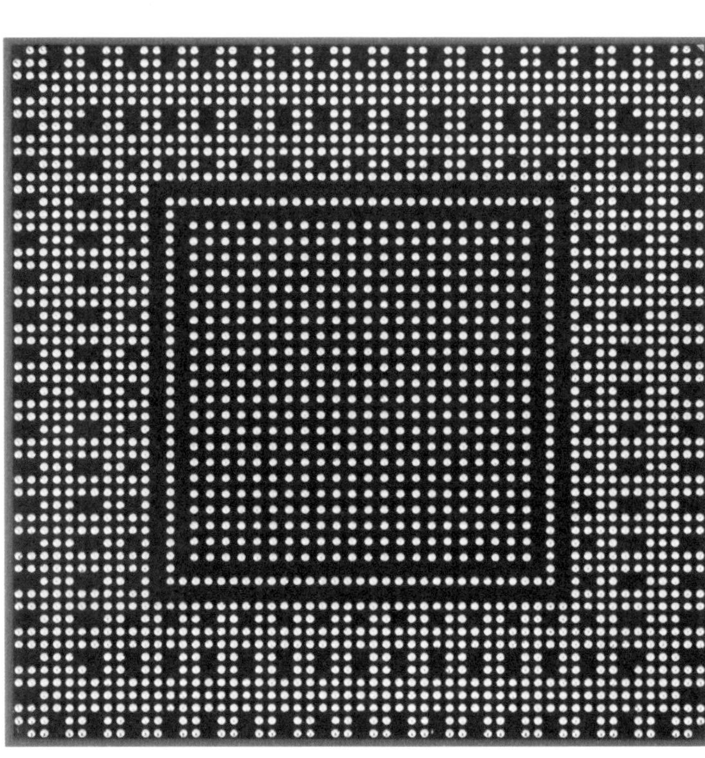

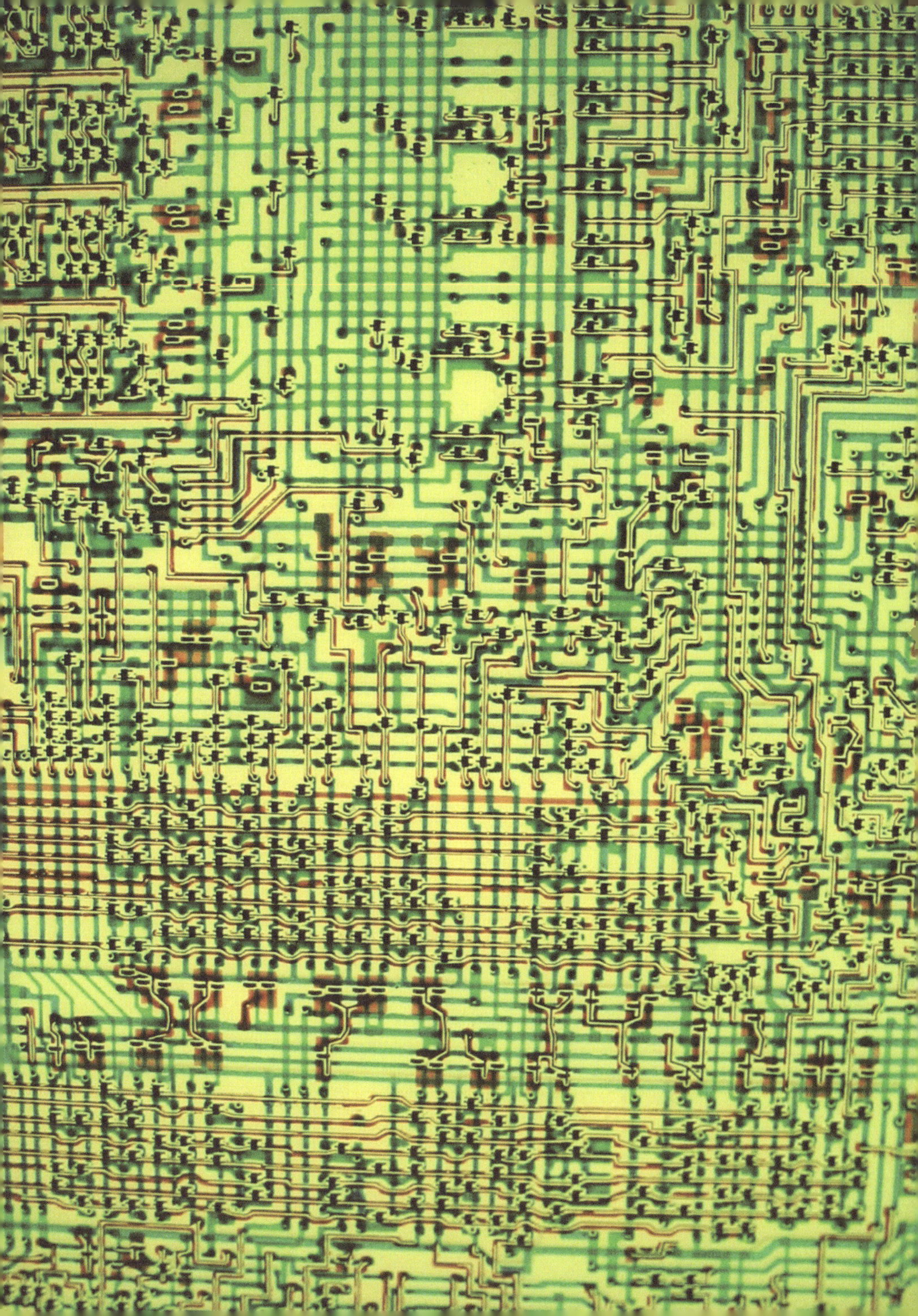

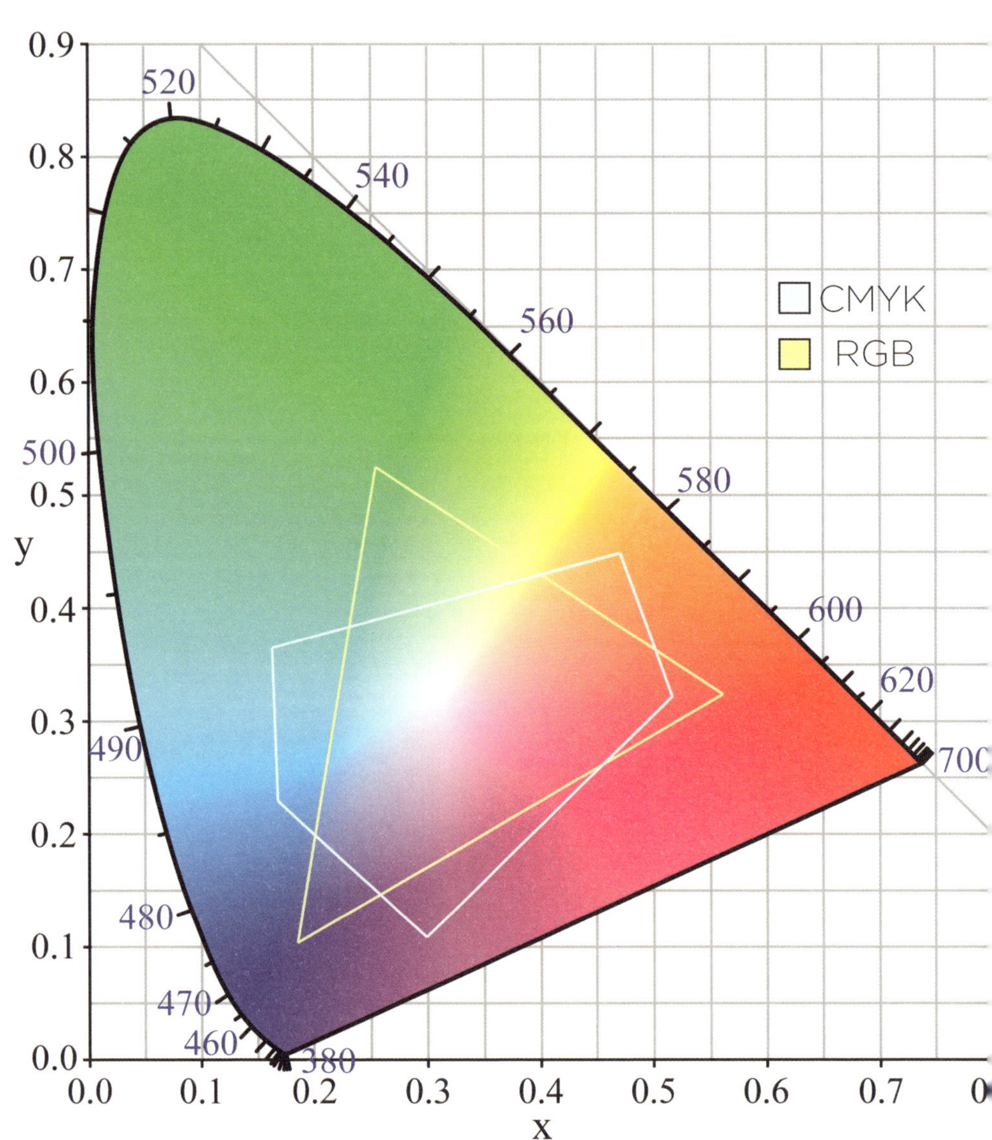

VISIBLE SPECTRUM
y
x
CMYK
RGB
0.9
0.8
0.7
0.6
0.5
0.4
0.3
0.2
0.1
0.0
0.0
0.1
0.2
0.3
0.4
0.5
0.6
0.7
520
540
560
580
600
620
700
500
490
480
470
460
380

A color model is an abstract mathematical model describing the way colors can be represented as tuples of numbers, typically as three or four values or color components e.g. RGB and CMYK a color model with no associated mapping function to an absolute color space is a more or less an arbitrary color system with no connection to any globally understood system of color

Adding a   mapping function between the color model and a   reference color space results in a definite "footprint" This "footprint" is known as a gamut and in combination with the color model defines a color space.

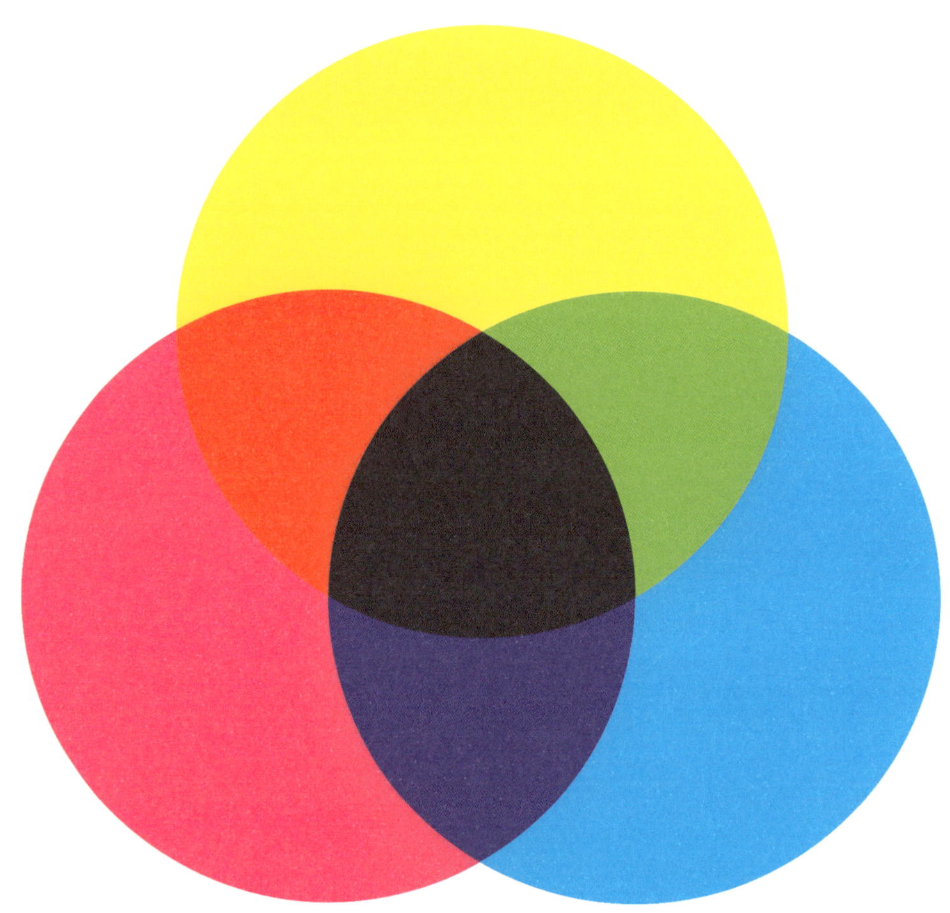

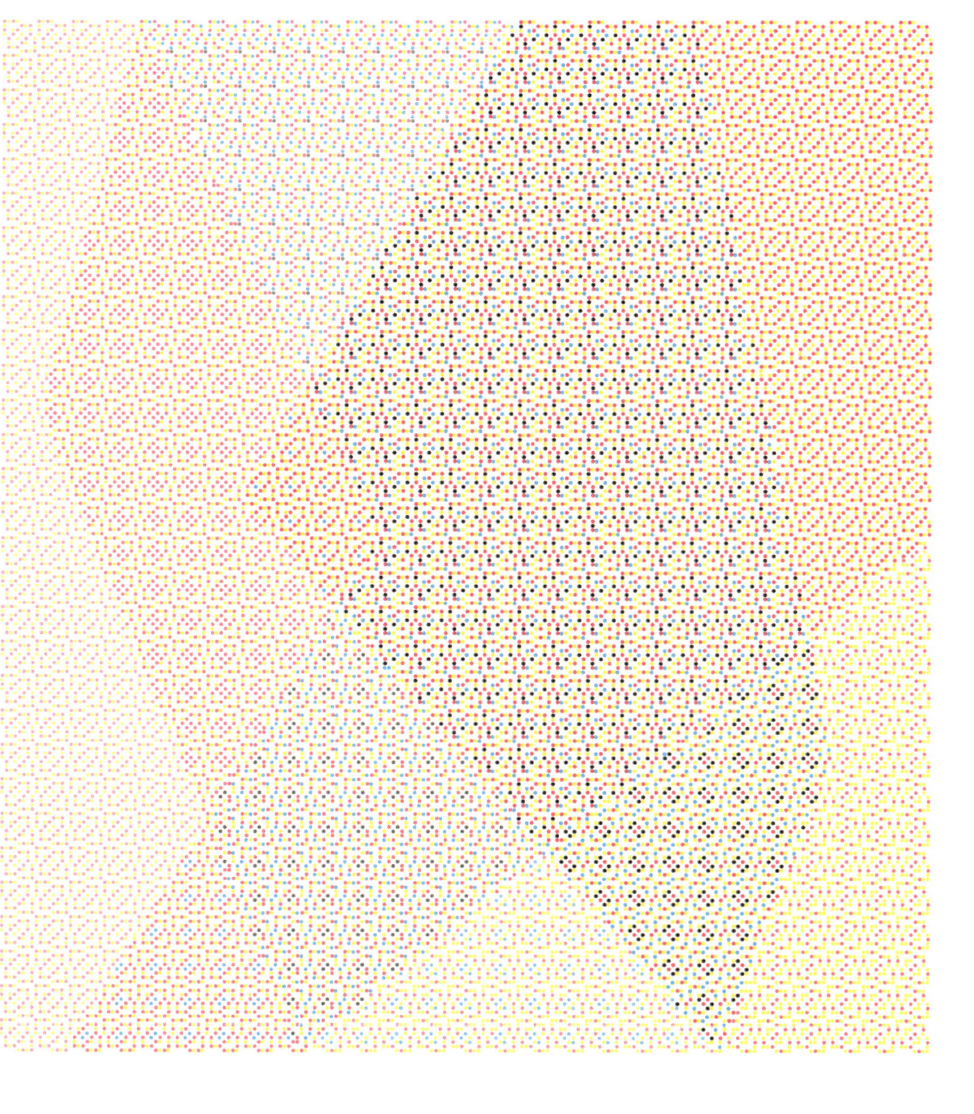

SOURCES REDACTED